Bo
Sp

'I admit that, from the age of sixteen, I have fancied both men and women. But sex has never been an obsession with me. However, I think I'll end up with a woman, because I would love to have children.' – *London Sunday Magazine*

'One day I could easily end up as a man with a pipe by the fireside.' – *London Daily Express*

'I don't think I look like a girl.' – *Melody Maker*

'I've had terrible relationships. Even now I have violence. I have terrible punch-ups with people. I need arguments. I need a sort of torrid relationship. I need to swear and smash things and cry – not in a defeatist way, but in a positive way.' – *New Musical Express*

'My first experience with a girl was with this girl called Brenda, who grabbed hold of me at my brother's party. I'd never kissed a girl and she kissed me. It was like, "Wow, I've kissed a girl, I've done it – now I can do it all the time." ' – *When Cameras Go Crazy*

'I've always dressed up. I've been doing it for years, and it's the way I've always got what I wanted. I've always had a great life. I've enjoyed myself, and I'm sure my life would have been a lot different if I hadn't had some sort of image or attraction.' – *Melody Maker*

'Obviously, I'm into myself, but I'm not walking around just saying, "Oh everybody look at me, look at me." ' – *The Face*

'Nobody creates things, everything you see is a complete rip-off of something else. If you're not influenced by everything, you must be a real moron.' – *Melody Maker*

'Most people don't want to be different, because it frightens them to be different, they've got this fear of alienation, of not being accepted. It's different with me because I couldn't give a toss, really.' – *The Face*

BOY GEORGE

'I think people in the U.S. think of me as very feminine. But I'm very masculine. I can throw a good punch. I'm taller and bigger than people expect me to be: I'm sure they expect a little fairy wearing dandelions. When we first went to Los Angeles, all these women were saying, "My God, you're so big!" as if they expected to see this midget getting out of the car.' – *Musician*

'I don't think clothes make the person. I think it's the personality, the character.' – Culture Club Press Conference

'Culture Club is very rooted in nostalgia. A lot of the best songs you hear – if you listen to them – sound like such and such a song. Yeah, we're definitely nostalgia freaks. We steal all our ideas.' – Culture Club Press Conference

'I'm not boring – at least, not in comparison. I mean, everybody else is much more boring than I am.' – Culture Club Press Conference

'I don't read books generally. The only book I've ever read was the story of Tallulah Bankhead – that was great fun.' – Culture Club Press Conference

'I always generally wear make-up. It's a personal thing. I just hate the look of my face without it. It's as simple as that.' – Culture Club Press Conference

'What's the difference between Culture Club and Van Halen? What's the difference between us and Kiss? What's the difference between us and Elvis Presley? There's no difference. I think the trouble is, we forget what's gone on in the past.' – Culture Club Press Conference

'I don't think Boy George is a passing fancy.' – Culture Club Press Conference

'I'd rather be like old Auntie Mavis at the wedding than be the serious young man. I like looking at paintings, but I don't like serious art. I like things you can touch. I like reality, old women with Mr Spock eyebrows. I like character – that's art.' – *Melody Maker*

BOY GEORGE

Merle Ginsberg

NEW ENGLISH LIBRARY

First published in the USA in 1984 by Dell Publishing Co. Inc.

First NEL Paperback Edition October 1984

NEL Books are published by
New English Library,
Mill Road, Dunton Green,
Sevenoaks, Kent.
Editorial office: 47 Bedford Square, London WC1B 3DP

Printed in Great Britain by Cox & Wyman, Reading.

British Library C.I.P.

Ginsberg, Merle
Boy George.
1. Boy George 2. Rock musicians——
England——Biography
I. Title
784.5′0092′4 ML420.B757

ISBN 0-450-05790-9

For my parents

Acknowledgements

I'd like to thank my extremely patient and understanding editor, Gary Luke – who both tolerates and dismisses idiosyncracy.

Also thanks for patience – Bob Mecoy, of Dell Books.

My friends and colleagues at MTV – Stuart Cohn and Jeff Peisch – were also instrumental in allowing me the space I needed to do this.

In fact, all of my friends helped by being understanding during the few months I was even more flipped out than usual: Jane Friedman, Susan Martin, Lou Stathis, Beth B, Robin Holland, Maureen Nappi.

Thanks to Beth Ginsberg and Cynthia Carst for excitement.

For continual interest, patience, and respect: the producers, and staff, of MTV Music Television.

And, for Bob Christgau: If you think I can write – then (maybe) I believe it.

This is what I learned, writing a book: Working hard, and concentrating on something outside yourself, keeps you from getting depressed.

Thanks to *NME* and *Melody Maker* for turning me on to Culture Club.

And special thanks to Boy George, for being 'fabulous.'

Contents

1

BOY WONDER

February 1984: French customs officials at Nice Airport are completely baffled this time. They've seen a lot of . . . *odd* types passing through international customs before – they've certainly seen a lot of suspicious types. But they've never seen anything like this.

The conspicuous party in question is a good six feet tall and decked out in the garb of a Japanese geisha girl: full-length blue and silver kimono with wide silk sash, past-shoulder-length dark locks, white face make-up heavily powdered, and Oriental-style slimming eyeliner. And, to make matters even more complicated, the party is accompanied by another party – a real Japanese woman who's also done up *à la geisha*, but who does seem to be the real thing (Japanese). Finally, the 'oddness' of the first character is revealed. The differences between geishas number one and two are *more* than racial. The tall Japped-out *femme* is trying to tell them she's an *homme*.

The party's passport does say he is George O'Dowd, citizen of Great Britain. But he goes even further than that, telling the officials, in a voice that's neither masculine nor feminine, that he's a singer – no, a 'pop star' – and that he's on his way to a gig at the giant San Remo music festival.

The echoing of snickers *en français* reverberates throughout the customs area. If he's so famous, why does his passport look nothing like him? And why have they never heard of him? But this 'George' fellow – or *whatever* he is – demands loudly to be allowed into the country at once. He doesn't understand that these middle-age Frenchmen haven't heard of him. He explains that he is internationally *famous* and that he is not at all amused by all of this. By now, very curious passers-by have gathered to watch this little tête-à-tête. Haven't they ever heard of Culture Club?

This gets George absolutely nowhere. The customs men have heard of many clubs, but not that one. They only want to know *one* thing – if this geisha is the man on the passport, *why* is he wearing '*une frock*' and '*le make-up*'?

'I am sorry, um, Monsieur O'Dowd,' an official says. 'We just cannot accept that you are *ze homme* pictured on your passport. I am afraid you will have to come wiz us . . . and prove it.'

Our Boy George isn't ruffled by threats of such an inquiry, nor is he particularly insulted. He's used to it – heard it all before – but he just wants to get the bloody hell out of Nice to San Remo, where thousands of fans are anxiously waiting for him. He flatly refuses to submit to any 'sex tests' and makes what seem like some rude jokes in English about the very idea.

So, he and friend Miko, a Japanese dancer and sometime rock journalist, are held up, arguing, for a good three hours. Then somebody gets the bright idea to call the British Embassy – where someone, though a bit amused, immediately confirms that this Boy is, indeed, a man. Or, at least, the Boy he claims to be. In fact, he may be the most famous Boy in the world.

Free at last, George and Miko, just a little worse for wear and tear, fly off to San Remo. But the Boy can't resist one last snicker of his own – particularly since a large crowd of reporters and photographers have now gathered. 'The *French* are certainly not going to stop me,' he sniffs. 'After all, the British and the Americans couldn't.'

And off he went, adding another triumph to an already long list.

The story of how George O'Dowd grew up and became a huge international pop star is not your average music business fairy tale. But then George is hardly your average pop star. Sure, Culture Club has sold millions of records around the world, and George has graced every magazine cover from *Rolling Stone* to *Newsweek* to *Salut!* (France) to *Okej* (Japan) in little more than two years. But he's also a man who likes to dress. Call it androgynous or effeminate; it's certainly *not* inconspicuous! It certainly *is* flam*boy*ant.

When he first appeared on the music scene in 1981, journalists described him as a 'Jamaican rabbinical student.' It was the peculiar combination of dreadlocks and vaguely religious-looking robes he wore. Just last winter *Rolling Stone* referred to George as a 'hulking youth who . . . wears more make-up than most premenopausal women this side of Miami Beach.'

Yet this same so-called gender-bender and most outrageous graduate of London's wild school of post-punk is making some of the sweetest, most soulful and melodic, lyrically emotional music this side of Smokey Robinson. Still, there is something inconsistent about this outlandish-looking fellow singing those romantic, charming, and *sincere* songs. Indeed, Boy George *is* what he sings: charming, warm, and sincere. He is also what he appears to be: outrageous, funny, bold, style-conscious. For his fans, he becomes that much more real for these incongruities.

'I see him developing into a chameleon character like David Bowie did in the seventies,' predicts top British DJ Mike Read. But George isn't cool or removed like Bowie, and he's never plotted away at his image or the superstardom he's achieved. George hasn't got a slick bone in his body. He carved out his own route in the confusing and overwhelming maze some call the music business by being true to himself and his own 'special' idea of what beauty is – a thing that comprises both his songs and his looks.

'He has the most soulful voice I've heard in years,' says Rod Stewart.

'The most outrageous character since Elton John and Liberace,' wrote the London *Daily Express*.

That Boy George; if there's one thing he is, both musically and physically, it's clever.

'He's a huge international star, and he's here to

stay!' That's how Joan Rivers announced Boy George to the audience of the American *Tonight* show in February 1984. A good deal of America was watching that night, waiting to see if Joan would pry untold secrets from her latest victim. After all, George offered more material than most for satire. However, it didn't turn out that way.

'I love what you're wearing,' she told him, of his wildly coloured quilted rags.

'This was a bedspread,' announced George. 'In Barcelona. I saw it – on a bed. In a shop. And I had to have it.'

'Which do you like – boys or girls?' Joan asked brazenly.

'You, darling!' George cooed.

'No, really,' she came back, more determined. 'If you were on a desert island, and all that . . . '

'You, darling.'

'No, *really*.'

'Well, either one,' George conceded blithely. 'I don't really have time to think about that these days.'

'Why do you wear make-up?'

'Oh, well, like Sheena Easton, I make the most of what I've got.'

By the time George took his bows, Joan Rivers was practically eating out of his hand. He'd fared well – quite well, in fact. Some say he stole the show from the guest who preceded him: Joan Collins. America's latest sweetheart was a Boy!

'He's changed the *face* of music in America,' said Culture Club drummer Jon Moss to *Rolling Stone*. 'He did, right? He opened the door. Duran Duran went there before us, but we actually opened the doors. I mean, imagine America accepting what, supposedly, to them, is a transvestite – but he's the biggest star in America at the moment, right? A guy who wears make-up, is effeminate, sings songs about men – WOW! Y'know, WOW! That's an achievement.'

No, George's ascent to American and worldwide household word-dom and Boy Wonderhood has not been typical or predictable. Maybe that's why, as Joan Rivers puts it, 'he's a star for the eighties.' George jumps the barriers few would have attempted or imagined crossing. For instance, Culture Club took *both* British and American recording industry top honours this year (the U.K.'s BPI awards and the U.S.'s Grammy for best new group). Then England's *New Musical Express* (*NME*) named George 'best dressed' in both the male *and* female categories!

Boy George's fans are both, surprisingly, romantic idol-craving teenage girls, who find him 'sweet,' 'sensitive,' 'fashionable,' and 'sexy' – *and* macho insecure teenage boys, who think he's 'daring,' 'brave,' 'funny,' and even 'pretty.' But it doesn't stop with teenagers. The hip, upwardly-mobile adult crowd also finds the music soothing and pleasingly reminiscent of the sixties' Motown. Then there are the parents, who actually *do* like the music and find George 'unthreatening,' 'nice, even,' and much less offensive than leather-and-stud-clad heavy-metal rockers and scary, nasty punk types.

But most surprising is the group that makes up George's favourite fans – the *grannies*. Grannies never dig grandkids' sounds, but they all seem to dig Boy George. 'I like it when I come out of a TV studio and see a lot of grannies there. They're so . . . nice,' says George. He won't forget that when the British press was criticizing him in 1982, the editors received letters begging, 'Leave him alone! He's really *lovely*.' One was signed 'Mrs Jones, age sixty-four, Swansea.' The grannies knew something about George before the rock press did – that at heart, he's extremely traditional. Moral, even.

After all, this is the Boy who admits, 'I think love and sex are very similar things – they go together. I don't think that I could now sleep with anyone unless I loved them. I think the feeling you have from having sex with somebody you love is far more exciting than having sex with somebody you don't know.' This is a far cry from the anarchistic punk sentiment of a few years earlier. As Boy George says, ' . . . for years, people in pop music have had this horrible illusion that sex symbols had to be really obvious, and I think I've come along at a good time.'

Culture Club's music spans more than just age groups. Stylistic, cultural, and race groups are bridged in this club. It's trendy but hardly exclusive. Says Jon Moss, 'People never feel alienated from Culture Club, which is a good thing. Spreading happiness and making people feel welcome is much better than going . . . "we're out to shock." That's much too easy.' The Club is purposefully inclusive – their songs are played on America's video station MTV, on album-oriented rock radio, on soul and disco radio formats, in Latin clubs, on Japanese dance floors. Maybe that's because, as George says, 'I like all music – so we use a bit of everything.' Culture Club is the first mainstream pop band to incorporate reggae, country, soul, and rock styles – while still sounding distinctive and modern. It's pretty impossible not to sing along with a Culture

Club song.

George's impact is larger than the musical one. No other rock performer or pop star, from the Beatles to Bowie, has influenced both avant-garde fashion fetishists *and* the mainstream vogue to such an extent. In the past, musical groups that incorporated a 'look' wound up with an audience trying to affect a bit of it and possibly having their style picked up by very trendy culture-vultures. It often took up to a decade before bands saw their styles trickle down to the mainstream.

The early eighties club-scene look in London wasn't really a pure one. In the mid to late seventies, it had been all leather and spikes and coloured hair. That ended when Spandau Ballet broke in 1980 with their first hit. They initiated a new and totally opposite look, called New Romantic which was about total escape and masquerade. The New Romantics, probably symbolized best by Adam Ant, wore pirate outfits, ruffles, capes – anything to look out-of-date, glamorous, larger than life, and unaffected by the depressed British economy. Right before Boy George appeared on the scene, you coud find the posers in the London clubs wearing just about anything; 'the look' had become an amalgam of counter-culture styles.

But when Culture Club broke with its first single, 'Do You Really Want to Hurt Me,' in late 1981, our Boy was decked out in his very own look – white smock with black and gold Arabic lettering, loose-fitting knickers underneath, rag-tied plaits of hair bound with scarves – all topped off with a wide-brimmed felt boater hat (now referred to as a generic 'Boy George' hat, even though he currently doesn't sport one). His look was not traditional, punk, nor bohemian. No one had ever seen anything like it. It escaped simple classification – hence descriptions like 'Hasidic Rasta.'

But faster than you can say 'dreadlocks,' trendies of both sexes were emptying the stores of any available gear to accomplish the look. Soon walking London streets were myriad variations of George, who came to be known as 'Boy George clones.' Of course, then the press got after the Boy for *that* too. He responded to those charges in London's *Melody Maker*: 'Look, I don't think individuality has anything to do with dressing up – it's got everything to do with *character*. A lot of people make the mistake of thinking that because somebody dressed up like them, they're not an individual – which is complete and utter rubbish, because when I see people at a concert looking like me, I see it as a flag-waving situation, I see them as mascots and I think it's very positive that they're *with* us. It's a bit like if you go to a peace demonstration and you take a banner. Most of them probably go back home to suburbia and take off all the make-up, but I don't care.'

Boy-inspired clothes started flying out of London in 1982, landing on the jet-set hangers at Bloomingdale's and Macy's and on L.A.'s Melrose Avenue. George's baggy-layered look (nicknamed by *Rolling Stone* 'the Bulgarian bag-lady look') was soon featured on the pages of *Vogue*, *Mademoiselle*, and *Women's Wear Daily*. Why does it have such appeal? A lot of people think it's asexual and unflattering. George loves this.

'We live in a society that's basically imperfect. One of the nicest things ever written about us was that we attract little fat girls who put belts around their shirts and who are aware that they're a bit podgy,' says Geoge. 'I've made that very fashionable in the sense that it's very androgynous, very sizeless, and you don't know quite what's going on under it. I love that bit of mystery.'

This year the young British designers are experiencing *their* long-awaited 'invasion' as well. The giant oversized 'Boy' look (and there's an American company called Boy making them) for shirts, pants, shoes, and hats, plus 'overcoloured' make-up are all the rage. It is accepted 'high fashion' from Kensington High Street to the pages of *The New York Times Magazine.*

But Boy George's most powerful effect – intended or not – has probably been in the delicate area of sexual tolerance. When his made-up face began gracing magazine covers across the world, all anybody really wanted to know about him was whether he was gay (or otherwise 'perverted') or *not*. And then, after that, they wanted to know with whom he was sleeping.

But as the world has grown more familiar with Culture Club's music, and George has become a fixture in the media, his ambiguous sexuality has taken a back seat to the music. This is quite incredible, considering the fight women's lib and gay lib have waged for just such tolerance. This is not to say that Boy George has come along and swept away the world's sexual prejudices. He's just refused to be pigeonholed into any stereotypes.

He keeps on surprising people by being *truly* idiosyncratic – an individual, with an individual talent. You can't say George dresses up like a girl – George dresses up like himself. He's that 'karma chameleon' in the song, never satisfied to stay the same from day to day, from song to song. But how much does that have to do with the way he *really* is? Just how our Boy George – once called 'The Thing' by repulsed journalists – has come into his own is not your average fairy tale at all.

2

BAD BOY

It was a bright Monday morning in 1976, and fifteen-year-old George O'Dowd felt like going to school – for a change. Like most of the kids his age, he didn't feel like that too often, but unlike most of them, he actually followed his whims. He'd been truanting more and more this term, to the point where he'd actually spent the whole of the last week sitting in the woods and walking around the streets, looking in the shop windows. That was somewhat better than school, but not all that much – none of the local shops in Eltham could offer any better fashions than he could whip up on his own from rubbish bins and second-hand stores.

He loved his latest look. It was sort of ted (short for teddy boy, the trendy London style from the fifties) and sort of 'Bowie' at the same time: bright orange-dyed hair (which Mum loathed but was afraid to criticize), cut in that new 'wedged' style; drainpipe trousers; a short, skinny tie (which he'd coerced Mum into cutting and sewing smaller); and white plastic sandals with platforms. He received lots of compliments from his mates, but his teachers were continually dragging him over the coals about it. He was sick of their attitudes and liked to add some new fancy bit to his attire whenever they complained about his going overboard.

He dressed in the usual way that Monday, surprised Mum by skipping his favourite breakfast – flakes in milk – and left for school. It didn't even occur to him that he was over an hour late. They ought to be quite pleased to see me today, he mused on the way.

Making his way up to his Special Needs Department on the top floor of Eltham Green School – the class for the 'special cases' – he bumped right into the headmaster. It was clear the headmaster was not as pleased to see him as he'd expected.

' "Why are you *late*?" ' George recalls the headmaster bellowing, in *When Cameras Go Crazy*.

' "I got up late," ' George replied honestly. There didn't seem to be any sense making excuses.

The headmaster was not impressed by this moment of candour. ' "Save your confessions for fools, boy," ' he went on. ' "I saw you on the High

Street on Friday – I'd recognize *that* hair anywhere. You haven't been here in a fortnight." '

George didn't deny that.

The headmaster began raising cane, literally. It was common punishment at this school, and at most English schools, for teachers to beat students with their canes – just to keep them in line, of course.

' "No way!" ' yelled George, jumping out of the way of the dreaded cane. ' "I don't have to take the cane off you. I don't want to be at this school. I don't like it, and I want to go home. I don't want to learn anything else." '

The headmaster was, for once, at a loss. He'd never seen a student like this one. He just didn't seem to care what happened to him, and his parents didn't have any effect on him.

' "Boy, I've got no choice if you continue in this manner but to expel you from this school." ' The words rolled off his tongue like thunder – it was the final ultimatum.

' "Fine," ' was what the Boy replied. And he turned to go.

George was greatly relieved, but he still had Mum to deal with. In a way, she should expect it, except he hadn't been giving her the warning letters the school addressed to his parents. They were fools for thinking he'd give them those letters and then submit to a beating. Would Mum punish him? Would she beat him? Would she let Dad beat him?

She didn't do any of that. She was dead tired of fighting with George. She came in with George when the school rang up and asked her to, but she was all quiet and resolute about it.

Of course, none of the school officials talked to George. They just addressed all the questions to his mother, as if his choice didn't exist.

Finally he remembers his mum turning to him and saying, ' "Right – well, do *you* want to come back, or not?"

' "No, not at all."

' "Are you going to work?" she asked him.

' "No, I'm not going to work."

' "Well," she said, turning back to the teachers and such, "he doesn't want to be here, so we might as well leave."

' "What do you mean?" ' they demanded – in George's opinion, quite stupidly, as usual.

' "We leave," she answered, and off they went.' They took the bus home. Mum was quiet and, it seemed, a bit sad. But she didn't say anything nasty. George didn't know how he felt – glad, he guessed, but also a bit worried. He didn't want to get a job, that would be awful. Well, he figured, something or other would turn up. Sooner or later.

Little did he know that that day in October 1976 was the first real step towards the future Boy's pop stardom.

Jeremiah and Diana O'Dowd were an average Irish-Catholic working-class couple living in a three-bedroom house in Eltham, in South London, with two sons, Richard and Kevin. Daddy Jeremiah had been a soldier and a boxer, but he now worked as a builder and was having a hard time making ends meet. Diana stayed at home with the kids and kept order in the small house that didn't have much – but it was kept up quite neatly. The whole family went to church every Sunday. It was quite a typical British domestic status quo. And no doubt Jeremiah and Diana intended it to stay that way.

Their third baby boy, George Alan, was born on June 14, 1961, and was soon followed by two more brothers (Gerald and David) and a wee sister (Siobhain, pronounced 'Shivann'). From that point on, there was a space problem in the Eltham house – what with all the boys sharing one smallish bedroom and little Siobhain getting most of Mum's attention. Domestic status quo went out of the window. George remembers it like this:

'When we were young, my father was quite strict. He had a lot of problems; he didn't have any money, he left the army, and he had all these bloody kids real fast. He was a builder, and he really had a hard time at it for years.'

What with six kids underfoot day and night, Jeremiah and Diana O'Dowd didn't have much time to show George the emotion he craved – at least that's what he claims, looking back on his childhood. He says he wanted to kiss his father good night, but that the senior O'Dowd would come home at night and just shout at the kids. The young George didn't take shouting sitting down – he was pretty ornery.

If his father yelled at him, George would just yell back. Now, in retrospect, he seems to regret those shouting matches. 'I was awful,' he told *Melody Maker*.

Yes, things got really wild in the O'Dowd abode. One day one of George's small brothers pulled his trousers down in church. Mum was so embarrassed that they never, ever, went back again. 'I was very pleased about that,' George remembers. But it only added to the internal tension.

Sometimes there was so much chaos in the packed house – so much chatter and sibling rivalry, so much laughter and loud music – that Jeremiah erupted and hit the first thing in front of him. And given the odds, that was often a small boy.

If Jeremiah would raise a hand to one of George's brothers, he would come to his defence – and get into big trouble himself. Somehow the concept of 'big trouble' that most kids come to associate with fights with their parents was missing from George's mind. He just didn't seem to care if he made his parents angry at him. He seldom seemed to feel guilty.

The only thing the boy George indulged in with his father was a bit of boxing. Jeremiah opened a boxing club when George was in his early teens, and he dragged his son along. George sort of liked boxing – but he didn't show much enthusiasm for it, because, as he now says, 'I knew I never intended to do anything that my father wanted me to.'

It wasn't much better between the boy and his mum. She had all the kids to look after and didn't have time to understand what was steadily becoming 'George's nasty temperament.' He wasn't at all like his brothers and sister – he demanded attention and then, when he *got* it, he'd be rude. She also couldn't understand just what it was about school that he hated so much, and why he did so poorly in it. He seemed bright enough.

He'd do anything *not* to have to go to school. He used a classic kids' trick, but one he pulled almost every day as a teenager. He'd eat his breakfast very slowly, until his mother would yell at him to hurry up. Then he'd try to act on her sympathy by claiming he'd throw up if he ate any faster. At first Mum would be sympathetic – but after days and days of George's missing school because he couldn't get out of the house fast enough, she wised up. Finally she took to screaming at him till he'd *have* to leave. Of course, he couldn't let the screaming go – he'd have to scream back, and a fight would ensue. Then, if he did go to school, the boy would spend all day wondering if she'd let him come home. Of course, she always did.

Yes, this boy was turning into a big problem – not just the victim of your average generation gap. He hated having no privacy at home; he hated his parents, his teachers, his school – and pretty much everything. Including, it seems, himself. He couldn't control what was now a really violent temper, and that surprised even him. (Years later he wrote a song called 'I'm Afraid of Me' that really captured the essence of his early teens. It was Culture Club's second single.)

But, luckily, as he marched reluctantly towards adolescence, George finally found something he didn't hate – music. And it didn't take long, with all that bottled-up emotion, for him to fall in love with it.

* * *

His older brother Richard had become a 'skinhead' (forerunners to punks), but George was drawn to that seventies phenomenon 'glitter rock' – hard rock performed by effeminately dressed boys. That brilliant movement was a much bigger trend in England than in America. But as Ray Davies of the Kinks observes, British kids are more 'dedicated followers of fashion,' in both music and clothes. In the U.K., bands with boring clothes are mostly doomed to second-rate status.

So George's first rock 'n' roll hero wasn't John Lennon or Eric Clapton or Jeff Beck – it was Marc Bolan, outrageous 'glam' star of the band called T-Rex. George liked Bolan's music, but he *really* flipped for his clothes – and did his own version of the 'glam' look by perusing second-hand shops and the Salvation Army for embroidered jackets, gauze shirts, and bell-bottoms with big appliqués. He also let his own hair grow long and insisted on curling it, like Bolan. Mum really cringed over *that* one. He didn't have money for clothes; he relied on ingenuity to put together his look. He loved his new identity.

He began dressing up to go *everywhere* – even Sunday school, where he often went in a big camel's-hair coat, floppy hat, platform shoes, bell-bottoms, and a neckscarf. The neighbours had a field day, and Mum hid.

Having got used to his temper, the O'Dowd parents now had to come to terms with George's new (and persistent) flam*boy*ance. They were as startled as any of the neighbours by it, but they also would do anything to fend off a temper tantrum. So they kept their comments to themselves. Anyway, there was no stopping George, as the Nice customs men later found out. Dressing up was the only thing that gave him pleasure and made him feel important. Got him a few comments and a lot of looks on the street.

At this point, after much complaining to the local housing council, the O'Dowds got to move into a bigger house a few miles north in an area of Eltham called Shooters Hill. George was a teenager. But things didn't improve much with the move. George and Dad were still going at each other's throats nightly. There were the usual everyday kind of squalls – and, occasionally, a really ugly incident.

When George was about fourteen – his most difficult stage – he gave up caring whether his father really loved him or not. That's when the fights got particularly bitter – and the fighting didn't end. But neither side could stand it anymore. George decided to flee to a neighbour's for a while, except he didn't bother to tell his parents that. Not just a wee while either – about a couple of weeks. But all he did was think about home, and his parents were in quite a state, missing him and feeling totally confused and rejected.

'I was quite lonely, because I really loved my mother, you know what I mean? I used to really get on with her on my good days. And I did like my dad too, because, believe it or not, I liked his attitude. I *like* people getting angry. I hate no emotion.'

Sure enough, George's mother, feeling quite miserable with him away from home, called him up at the neighbour's and begged him to come back. Being as dramatic as he is, George declined. Then his father got on the line and asked him to come back, saying everything would be okay.

'And I went back, and it *was* fine. It was really weird, but my dad changed completely from that day on. And now – he's brilliant. It's weird, but I *can* kiss him now. I couldn't when I was a kid – and that sort of thing, you really want to do it when you *can't*, know what I mean?'

It was during this prophetic period of adolescence that George also fell on another thing he could like: *girls*. He thought them sharp, funny, more understanding and encouraging than his mates. An the ones he liked – the really smart-looking ones who were a bit *bad* – also seemed to like him quite a lot. His first crush was on the most outrageous girl in his class, Tracie Birch. Everyone had a crush on her – she had a green Vidal Sassoon haircut (coloured hair had much wider acceptance in the U.K. than it ever did in the U.S.) and really knew how to dress and who the good groups were. It was Tracie who instigated George's stylistic transformation of 1975, which led to the orange hair and drainpipe pants. She seemed to really like to dress him up, and he was more than willing to comply. She also let him try her make-up. All the while he liked Tracie, he went to school more often, so he could see her as much as possible.

But the school authorities were much less lenient about George's excessive appearance than his parents. When the headmaster (the same one who later expelled him) got his first glimpse of the orange hair, George recalls he stopped and asked, 'What do you think you are – a *belisha beacon*?' George did not know what a 'belisha beacon' was, but he knew it wasn't exactly a *compliment* on his stylish aesthetics. 'I don't know what *you're* complaining about,' sniffed the boy. 'You've got on a gown and a board with a tassel!' (English headmasters regularly don the garb Americans reserve for graduation exercises.)

George, it was decided, was a problem case. He

definitely had problems at school, and he definitely *was* a problem. He was banished to the 'problem class' in the small attic of the suburban school, with a school therapist as teacher – or baby sitter, really. The room was called the Greenhouse, and the boy was to be under constant surveillance. He was allowed only to read or draw – nothing else. He chose to truant.

George looks back on his school days now with a clear undestanding of why it couldn't work for him. 'At school, the attitude is basically one where they try to destroy your personality – it's much easier to teach twenty people to think the same than nineteen – and one that doesn't. I think a lot of people can bow down to that pressure, but *I* can't. I found it impossible.'

And sure enough, within months it proved to be just that. At age sixteen he was free and on his own.

3

DRESSING TO BE CLEVER

It was just your average night during the dawning of the burgeoning London club scene, circa mid-seventies. If you observed the decor (basement), the outfits (black leather), and the haircuts (spike city), you might have described it as punk. But *that* term didn't exist yet. Insiders called it fun. Outsiders called it trendy. All their parents called it disgusting.

George O'Dowd thought Bangs – the hottest and freakiest club in London (that week) – was the best place he'd ever found. He loved the way people looked there – especially this one bloke, who held most of the room's attention.

The interesting bloke was dancing, by himself (Billy Idol's recent hit 'Dancing With Myself' was released around this period), wearing what can only be described as a 'pre-punk' ensemble: horns on his head, a skirt, pit boots, black leather gloves, a black paper collar (for that 'reverent' touch), and black lipstick (for that 'irreverent' touch). He was dancing around in all that, and George immediately was sure he was the hippest guy in the scene. George aspired to that status.

The future Boy George spotted him again the next week at another, similar club called Louise's. This time the fellow was decked out in a jacket with candy wrappers all over it, an enormous top hat, suspenders, and to top – or bottom – it all off, shorts. However, he didn't stay in *that* outfit all night – he changed his clothes right on the dance floor, carrying a bag of items with him when he danced.

George spotted him once more on the momentous and historic occasion of the Sex Pistols' first gig (the night some people will tell you punk was born). This time the guy was wearing hot pants and high heels, and acting as DJ – spinning songs from 'The Sound of Music' and other inappropriate records. Not exactly standard stuff.

George felt compelled to introduce himself to this person, who turned out to be Philip Salon, a well-known club personality. He thought Philip might snub him, but quite the opposite – and Philip was quite the opposite of the way he looked. They became best friends, sharing a mutual obsession with clothes and make-up and dancing. Philip became George's role model and guide through the labyrinth of the London underground. He was the perfect boy for our Boy – outrageous but moralistic. He and George are still close friends, and George counts him as one of his nearest and dearest.

George speaks fondly of him in *When Cameras Go Crazy*. 'He gave me a lot of confidence, which I didn't have in those days. He hates violence, and he doesn't lie. I think I've got quite a lot of my attitudes from him . . . . He doesn't skip his train fare – and then, he's weird, as well.'

It was mostly through Philip that Boy George became assimilated into the London club scene. Finally he had some direction.

'When I left school, I made the decision that I didn't really want to have a job,' George now says of that period. 'I'd started dressing up, and I thought, "If I go out and get a job, I'm gonna go dressed up. If I don't get the job, to hell with it." My parents were really against that – it was kind of "Do something to get a job, and *then* dress up." '

But George didn't really want a job anyway – the clubs took up all of his time. The travelling time from Eltham to London's Waterloo Station was about forty-five minutes each way, and he'd stay out *quite* late, sleep in the next day, and spend the rest of it finding clothes and trying them on.

He'd go to Shaguarama's, Louise's, the Global Village, the Goldmine on Canvey Island, the Black Prince, Bexleyheath, anywhere where a club scene might be brewing. He also frequented the gay clubs, because they were the trendiest of all.

George didn't go to the gay clubs because he considered himself gay or wanted to meet gay men or women. Everybody who was into dancing and dressing up went to these clubs, as easily as they went to their local pubs. Actually, the way most of these people looked, they were not always welcome at their local pubs – and the gay bars were a lot more tolerant. When people would come on to George in a gay club, he wouldn't insult them – but he never took it seriously. He thought the whole thing was funny and liked the 'taboo' aspect of it. He'd stay out all night and tell his mother he was staying at a friend's.

George does not say whether or not he actually *did* go home with any of the people he met at this period, but he does say this:

'Why does someone like me go to a gay club? For *laughs* – I mean, I don't relate to it, I don't believe people should live their sexuality. All these things, they're experience. It's amazing that the world is so small, and we're all so naive. I think if you can learn a few things, by mistakes and also by just living a bit, you know, it's great.'

In 1983, in an interview with a London daily paper, George announced this: ' . . . from the age of sixteen, I have fancied both women *and* men. But sex has never been an obsession with me . . . . I've slept with girls and blokes, but sex is not an obsession with me. It's like eating a bag of crisps – quite nice, but nothing marvellous.'

Of course, George has added, subtracted, and rewritten his views on this subject a thousand times since, but it's pretty clear that it was in his late adolescence, after he'd quit school, that he began to consider the issue of sexuality and question and experiment with his own. But he still had girl friends. There are tons of photos – snap-booth photos – of George with various girls. One, Shelley Hughes, he called his favourite. She was his longest-lasting girl friend. She taught him a lot about make-up and clothes.

So what was George wearing at this time? All sorts of things. Sometimes he wore shirts with suspenders and a *Night Porter*-looking armyish hat, and he'd pad his shoulders with socks. He had his hair cut so he could spike it up a bit, but also wore a lot of different hats.

'It was basically a Bowie thing,' George says of the atmosphere of the times, both in clothes and clubs. 'When Bowie was around, and Bryan Ferry, everybody used to go and see them. When Bowie came back from America, we all went to see him at the station, and you didn't realize how many weird people there were until you were there.'

It was 1976, and glitter rock was still trendy, but something else was brewing – *punk.* At the age of fifteen, George met a fellow named Troy who ran a clothing store called Shades. It was part of the Chelsea Antique Market – mostly glorified stalls on the trendiest street in London, the King's Road. (To this day, tourists go to the King's Road to take pictures of weird punks and outrageous dressers. The kids who 'pose' there charge money to have their pictures taken. That's the only livelihood they have.)

George got a job at Shades. It wasn't as punk as a lot of the other trendy clothes shops – like the one called Sex, which was started by Malcolm McLaren (who was about to launch another project, the Sex Pistols) and Vivienne Westwood, the now well-known fashion designer. (Sex later changed its name to World's End and became a fashion influence all over the world.) Shades sold thirties-looking suits and avant clothes for punk hold-outs.

George didn't hate working at Shades at all. He got his pick of clothes, was *very* gregarious with the customers, and met some great people – like Bob Marley, who was friendly with the owner. Ska music – reggae with a bit of British rock and a faster beat – was happening in the clubs, the Specials had formed, and everybody in London was buying reggae records. George, never one to miss a trend, also got into reggae, and loved talking to Bob Marley and the way he looked. Perhaps this is where his love of island looks and plaited hair began.

He also met a lot of his future influences at Shades. One day a boy with very curly hair told George, 'I like your hair' (it's impossible to pinpoint what it looked like at this exact time, because George changed hairstyles – and colours – sometimes daily). George said, 'I like *your* hair,' and the two formed a friendship on the basis of hair. The curly-haired one turned out to be Jeremy Fantayzee (not his real name, but the only one he'll acknowledge), who later formed the band Hayzi Fantayzee and changed his name to Jeremiah, after George's father.

George took Jeremy to parties, and vice versa – and between the two of them, they met everybody who was hanging out in London. The hanger-outers weren't working people, or entertainment business people. They were kids or would-be pop stars, or independent fashion designers, or people who had nothing better to do than dress up. Most of them had absolutely no ambitions whatsoever, except possibly 'to be famous.' But few of them had ideas on how to achieve it.

George began dressing as a 'teddy boy.' Teds weren't pretty or particularly glamorous. Standard ted fare was greased-back hair (preferably with Brylcreem, though Tenax is very popular now) swept into what are still called quiffs (front fluffs) and duck's arses (slicked tails); long jackets and drainpipe trousers – it was all loosely based on Elvis Presley. George dyed his coloured spiked hair and greased it into a quiff that fell four inches down his forehead, into his eyes. He drew on a moustache and wore brocade second-hand jackets. He out-tedded all the teds.

He left Shades to work at Tesco's, but was fired after a week because of the way he dressed. It took attention away from the goods on sale! As with his school expulsion, George didn't care about being fired. He only cared about the clubs.

And the clubs were getting more and more punk – 'suddenly you started getting punched in the mouth when you went out' – and the teds weren't welcome there. Bands like the Sex Pistols, the Damned, the Clash, the early Adam and the Ants (a punk band at that time), were taking over, getting violent on stage, and inciting the fights that took place offstage. George never liked the punk scene, thought it 'too angry' and ugly to look at. At the encouragement of his new friend Martin Degville (who'd influenced George's ted look with his own enormous quiff and moustache), George left London in 1977 (at the age of sixteen) and moved to Birmingham, to share a flat with Martin – and whatever girls happened to pass through town.

Martin wanted to design clothes and 'make a killing.' He opened a stall in a Birmingham market called Oasis, and George gave him its title: Degville's Dispensary. He and Martin went out *every* night and had no trouble attracting *all* the attention on the Birmingham club scene – they were not willing to settle for anything less.

A year later, when George got tired of the Birmingham crowd, he returned to London, now a more or less established club circuit star. He decided to take it all the way and get the kind of royal treatment he'd got in Birmingham – he was almost never satisfied with anything less than *all* the attention. He called up everybody and met everybody else who'd come to avant-prominence in the year he'd been gone.

The first new friend he made was someone called Marilyn – a boy. Marilyn, regarded by some as a transvestite, by others as yet another member of the growing group of London gender-benders, is now making his living as a pop star. 'When I first met him,' George remembers, 'he was a right little wally. And the next time I saw him, he had a dress on, a stuffed padded bra, crimped long hair and eyelashes – he was simply outrageous.' Marilyn, who got a major record contract last year (and some say more for sensationalism than talent), claims that he and George were romantically involved in 1978, but George won't acknowledge that. It seems that both Jeremiah and Marilyn believe George has turned his back on them ever since he's become quite successful. But they in turn have also basked in his success – attracting record company attention by being 'friends of Boy George.' Although the rivalry has been quite intense in the last year, particularly between Marilyn and George – Marilyn very deliberately saying he thinks he's as talented as George (but hardly proving it) – George went everywhere with Marilyn in 1978.

'Everywhere' at that point had changed a bit from the time George left for Birmingham. Night-lifers were tired of the aggression of punk. Most of the London punks didn't feel half as nasty as they *looked* – in leather, ripped T-shirts, studded belts, studded boots, spiked hair, and safety-pinned ears (and even *faces*). The bands that spawned punk got a bit tiresome performing the same violent dissonance continually. Most of the punks really just wanted to have *fun* and go out and would have been at the vanguard of *any* underground youth movement. English punk was more a fashion movement than a political one, and in 1978, it became a little more obvious about that.

And the independent fashion designers had a lot to do with it. They were tired of the drab punk looks and took punkishness to an extreme in their designs – going completely *outrageous* with studded dresses, leather everything – most of it looking more costume than anything else.

George and Marilyn started going to a new club now considered the cradle of the movement called the New Romanticism; it was called Billy's and was run by the progenitors of New Romantic music and fashion, Rusty Egan and Steve Strange. Both were very young, very hip, and *very* fashion-conscious. Rusty did what he did best at Billy's: disc jockeying, playing not nasty punk records but electronic funk music – and everybody danced like they hadn't danced in years (punk dancing was basically just jumping straight up and down – pogoing – or diving into other dancers – slam dancing). Steve donned a thousand varieties of weird costumes, wore brown make-up all over his face, and played the role of greeter at the door. Only London's *trendiest* were given entrée, and people – even punks – dressed up just to get past Steve's fastidious (and snobby) eye. Needless to say, George and Marilyn were on the permanent guest list.

Billy's became so popular that Rusty and Steve started their own electronic band called Visage (a perfect name, since it was all about Steve's many faces) and opened a bigger, trendier club, called the Blitz, in 1979. They coined the term New Romanticism for their *kind* of music and dress up, and the press – and the punks – picked up on it.

George, always in the vanguard of fashion, came into his own now. He sprayed his dyed-black hair and teased it so it stood straight up and straight out – like he'd got his finger caught in an electric socket. He went all the way and shaved his eyebrows, then painted on new ones in all kinds of shapes. He also started wearing heavy, brightly coloured eye make-up, dark lipstick, and brownish cheek blush. It was inspired by Steve Strange's look, but George discovered he had a good hand for make-up and even taught some of the New Romantic women – clothes designers like Melissa Caplan – how to do *their* hair and make-up. His clothes became more flamboyant than they'd ever been – blouses with enormous sleeves, giant smocks, huge cowl necks. Many of the designers gave him clothes and even used him as a model. George became quite good buddies with designer Steven Linard, who really added New Romantic images to his clothes – giant white poet collars on blouses, baggy velvet knickers and jodhpurs, enormous hoods, and gold chains on everything, often with big crucifixes dangling on the end.

New Romanticism took on a credo after it was born in the clubs – it was about exaggerated dress up, fun, dancing, and not taking *anything* seriously. The crucifixes and religious and pirate-looking costumes were attempted irreverence for everything, and adventure – even in the face of extraordinary British unemployment. New Romanticism took over from punk as *the* English youth movement in 1979, and George was one of its biggest spokespersons. Modelling the clothes, he even turned up on the pages of pop and fashion magazines in England.

'I was basically just going out at night, enjoying myself – getting drunk, doing whatever I wanted to do. Then, when I got about seventeen, I was getting in a lot of magazines. I'd started becoming a minor *celebrity*, really, and I was aware of that. I used to go home and my father would have bought a magazine somewhere and he'd say, "*You're* in this magazine" – but he could never work out *why*. He couldn't understand what was going on, whether I was part of a movement, or, y'know, part of the Socialist Party or something. He'd say, "George, what's going on?" And I'd say, "Oh, it's just because of the way I look" – it never dawned on him that this could be possible.

'Then I started to be in the dailies, in the *Sun* and the *Mirror*, and it became very odd. I had no money. I lived in a squat in London, and my parents couldn't understand why I was in newspapers. Y'know – "Why is my son in the paper when he lives *there*? What does he *do*? *What* is his career?" Y'know, that's what parents care about, how you live and how you eat. It was quite funny,' George told *Melody Maker* in 1983.

'Anyway, I got to the age of seventeen and I thought, "Okay, I want to *do* something now. . . . I decided I wanted a career, something that I really would enjoy.'

George got lucky – he'd done so much work with fashion designers and had got so good at changing his look that the Peter Benison modelling agency in London signed him up! This didn't give him any vanity about his looks (which he's always regarded with more than a bit of humour); it just helped him make some money, and he enjoyed it. He was featured as a sharp young New Romantic in ads for British Airways and the Trustee Savings Bank. George put the outfits together himself. He thought of the whole thing as a bit of a lark, but he liked the attention the ads received. He *did* begin, however, to take his talents as a stylist more seriously – designing hair, make-up, and matching clothes to models and to accessories – especially when he started to get offers from all directions to do it.

The best offer came from the Royal Shakespeare Company (a veritable British institution, where many of the great British actors – like Albert Finney, Diana Rigg, Richard Burton, Derek Jacoby, among others – began careers). A friend of George's with the somewhat accurate name of Mad Jean knew someone who worked at the Royal Shakespeare Company. When they needed a stylist to re-create for them 'an authentic punk look' for a play called *Naked Robots*, George O'Dowd was heartily recommended.

To get the right costumes, George approached a shop called Street Theatre. The store was in the business of renting costumes, but George managed to get them for free. Peter Small, the owner, was a *bit* resistant, but agreed, after George promised to get Street Theatre mentioned in the Royal Shakespeare Company programme.

George was interviewed about his theatrical experience in one British paper, and this is what he said: 'I used to be so rough with the actors – like a footballer. And I made all the women look like drag queens. They hated it, but I like drag queens.'

While George was beginning to make a go of his budding career in the fashion world, the London *Daily Star* snapped his picture for a 'stranger-than-fiction' photo feature called 'Weirdies!' The caption read: 'FLAMBOYANT: George O'Dowd, 19, wears Chinese slippers . . . old school trousers he tapered himself, and leg warmers. A black crepe Twenties dress – (fifty pence) from Oxfam – is pinned around his waist. Various tassel belts were picked up for a few pence, as were the long scarf and Oxfam beads round his neck. He got the large wooden cross from a friend, the crimplene blouse from his mum. A black felt hat and assorted earrings round off the outfit.'

This was the beginning of the look George made famous when Culture Club first exploded on the scene a few years later – his hair was long, and he wore it in little plaits with rags tied in, under a big black hat.

Peter Small of Street Theatre liked George's style and liked the publicity he'd got for his shop. So when the RSC job came to an end and George was broke again, Peter hired him to be the shop's dresser. Through Peter, George had another of his prophetic meetings – with a young dress designer named Sue Clowes. At first, George wasn't too wild about her clothes, but then he saw some fabric prints she did that he *really* liked. They got on well, and had a lot of mutual ideas about what looked good and what New Romanticism was all about. Peter Small got wind of this and decided to set the two of them up in a shop of their own around the corner, in Ganton Street. They called it the Foundry – and it later founded the look that helped launch Boy George's stylish career.

His looks were definitely not keeping him from his work – they had, in fact, *become* his work.

4

CULTURE SHOCK

In 1980, the New Romantics suddenly found out they were important. Their clothes – ruffled blouses with giant cuffs and collars, gold brocaded plus-fours, kilts, hooded capes, pirate looks with enormous pirate hats and Pilgrim-type shoes, plus anything *gold* – were turning up in fashion magazines and on the streets of London – and not just the trendy streets.

The New Romantics, just like the punks, had turned the politics of the avant-garde into real economic power for themselves. The movement swept its bands into local, then national, and eventually international, stardom – two of the biggest being Spandau Ballet and Duran Duran. They sure didn't look or sound like they do now, with millions of records behind them and years of touring.

Both Spandau and Duran sported longish curly

hair (very Elizabethan) and wore kilts, ruffled shirts, make-up, gold chains, and crucifixes. The music they played was in complete contrast with their almost Shakespearian-looking outfits: They produced funky electronic dance sounds that pulled together soul sounds with the new rhythm-machine noises.

The themes of the songs were other-worldly, dramatic: Duran Duran's 'This Is Planet Earth' (their first single) made the earth seem strange and inhuman. Spandau's 'Musclebound' was about adventure and story-book manhood. Adam Ant dressed up in the most exaggerated pirate gear, even wearing Indian-inspired make-up; all his songs with the Ants (before he went solo) were about walking the plank, high adventure.

Steve Strange and Rusty Egan were doing equally well with the Blitz (where all these bands congregated, danced, and played) and with the band Visage – which also put out electronic dance songs with a really eerie feel. Strange's look became more and more strange with the amount of publicity he received. He began to wear whiteface, and black lipstick, looking increasingly like some kind of odd doll (one of the first Visage songs was aptly called 'Mind of a Toy').

It was all pure *escapism*, and the complete

opposite of punk. Anybody who dressed normally was completely out of it. Yet, somehow or other, you hardly ever saw anybody dressed in this manner walking down London streets in the *daytime*. That's because the Cult of No Name – the bands, their followers, their designers – slept all day. At night they congregated in their clubs. None of the bands seemed to have any interest in commercial success, record company deals, or even press. They lived only to be trendy.

Back in America, no one had any idea such a thing was afoot. Reggae-inspired bands like the Specials and Madness were starting to break there, but both New York and Los Angeles were quite embroiled in their own little post-punk scenes and had little interest in London. American radio was showing its age, playing dying heavy-metal bands, middle-of-the-road rockers, and stadium groups like Styx, Foreigner, and Journey. The New Romantics might never have got any attention there – might never even have been heard, let alone seen – had it not been for one thing: the well-timed dawning of the rock video clip.

Meanwhile, George O'Dowd, who spent so much time on the music scene anyway, thought it might be *fun* to be in a band. His friend Kirk Brandon (who's now in a band called Spear of Destiny) wanted to start one. The two were living together in a small London flat. Kirk could sort of play bass, and he and George had another friend named Suede who was good enough on guitar. They got a friend named Luke to play drums, and called the band In Praise of Lemmings. Extremely dramatic. Very exaggerated. Up-to-the-minute.

George recalls, 'It was a real shambles, very much like a dirge. The music was very kind of political, very heavy, very sexual, the words were very Jean Cocteau – very young in a sense, very studenty – although I've never been a student.'

They had fun at rehearsals, but George in particular didn't take any of it seriously. He tried singing a bit, but it was all a way of showing his peers in the clubs that he was just as glamorous, if not more so, than they were. It was also a way of remaining a permanent guest at any of the clubs. George had no belief in the band, no belief in himself as a singer – so much so that one night, he put on a straw hat and stiletto heels, got thoroughly drunk, and approached Malcolm McLaren about being a part of his new 'project.'

McLaren was probably the only real entrepreneur in the whole of the London underground, with the World's End clothes shop selling the first punk clothing. Then he organized the first punk band, the Sex Pistols, by finding the scruffiest, least ambitious, most-unlikely-to-succeed individuals and making them a media sensation (and writing all the words and music for their controversial anarchistic songs). (McLaren himself became a recording artist last year, releasing his first album, called *Duck Rock*.) In any case, rumours were flying on the scene that McLaren was looking for flamboyant types – talented or not – to be in a new project, a New Romantic fashion band called Bow Wow Wow.

McLaren had already hired Matthew Ashman to be a guitarist with Bow Wow Wow. Ashman's girlfriend was someone named Gabriella, who was an agent for models and who'd signed up George to Peter Benison's agency. Matthew knew George and had heard him sing a bit, so he and Gabriella set about to convince Malcolm to give George a place in Bow Wow Wow.

'They wanted an effeminate guy originally – not like me, but sort of a bronzed Adonis type. They couldn't get one, so they got Annabella as a last resort,' recalls George.

Annabella Lwin was a fourteen-year-old London-Burmese girl whom McLaren had overheard singing in a dry cleaner's store where she worked. He decided to go for the nubile-schoolgirl image for the band, but after he hired her, he found out she wouldn't be as easily manipulated as he'd hoped. She was also not picking up the singing as quickly as McLaren wanted, so he agreed to bring in George for a try – hoping, really, that he'd frighten more co-operation out of Annabella. 'At the time,' says George, 'I thought he was doing me a favour, but actually he was doing *himself* a favour.'

McLaren gave George the name Lieutenant Lush and made him co-vocalist with Annabella. After some volatile rehearsals, George's career with Bow Wow Wow began – and ended – with a performance at London's Rainbow theatre. George earned good notices in the English music press, but then Malcolm turned around and cancelled Bow Wow Wow's first major tour in Britain. Really pissed off, George severed his relationships with everybody in the group. He blames it all on jealousy and personality conflict.

He told the press that Bow Wow Wow members Dave Barbarossa and Le Gorman never liked him because they found him too confident – and that McLaren never liked him either. 'He wasn't into the *idea* of me. He has to have people around him that he can channel his energy through; he has to have dummies that he can pipe up with his ideas, and it didn't really work with me,' George now claims. McLaren, it seems, didn't find George *funny*, and the Boy couldn't tolerate *that*. He also didn't find him particularly *sexy* – a necessary element in McLaren's grand scheme for Bow Wow Wow. He couldn't tell if the Boy was androgynous or sexless. He just wasn't sure how the public would take to him.

Now George's attitude on the whole thing is pretty philosophic: 'So it didn't work out, but it was a real experience for me, because I became involved with somebody who was quite a celebrity, and there were a lot of people writing about me. I became the subject of gossip.' Apparently George didn't mind this at all – and it's obvious now, he's always dealt with it well.

A London daily ran a photo of Annabella (in full pirate costume by Vivienne Westwood) and George (looking *très* New Romantic, in a poet's blouse and his hair up), with this caption under it: 'This terrifying apparition on the right is George O'Dowd, sometime singer with Bow Wow Wow (until manager Malcolm McLaren fired him), and now leader of a new band. George's problem is that everyone thinks he's a girl. "My mother wouldn't like that," pouts George, age twenty. "But when I went on stage during a gig with Bow Wow Wow in Manchester, everyone thought *I* was Annabella (the fifteen-year-old singer) and the boys were grabbing at me. I really don't dress up as a woman – I just like looking feminine." '

To this day, George vehemently disagrees with the notion that Malcolm McLaren really started his singing career: 'The one thing I want to stress now is that Malcolm McLaren never had anything to do with Culture Club,' he said in a recent interview. 'He didn't want me to be in Bow Wow Wow, Matthew Ashman (guitarist) wanted me. Malcolm thought I was a stupid New Romantic, so it's not like I was ever one of his protégés.'

So George went back to working in the Foundry, but by now he had discovered that he *liked* performing and that some people actually thought he was good. And he liked singing – it made him feel good. But, most of all, he basked in his new celebrity. Everyone wanted to know what he was doing next, what band he'd join, or if he'd start his own.

Kirk, on the other hand, was not so pleased with George's sudden quasi-musical notoriety. He really wanted to be a musician, and he started a sort of gothic punk band called Theatre of Hate. It was overblown, pseudo-negative, and much harder-edged than any of the New Romantic dance bands.

George didn't like the idea of it. He really couldn't get behind anything negative.

'I became very unfriendly with Kirk,' says George. 'I actually felt very sorry for him. I used to walk round with him when he took cassettes to places–telling people "Theatre of Hate blah blah blah," and these agencies and managers used to say "Oh, give up, it's useless." But I'd respect him for keeping on. He gave me a lot of my attitudes in that way, because I went round after that taking pictures of Culture Club, telling people this and that.' George managed to get Theatre of Hate some gigs because of his own influence in the clubs. But once this band got some recognition, Kirk started acting differently towards him. At that point, George stopped helping him, and their friendship dissolved.

'Anyway, they were really into punk rock, and that killed them, so I went off and got on with my own thing. I got this call in the squat from someone named Ashley Goodall at EMI Records, who said, "Blah blah blah, do you want to have a meeting? I was still really naive, so I said, "What about?" – and he said, "You're a singer, aren't you?" and I said, "Not now, I'm not in a band." So he said, "Well, you could be a solo artist . . . "

'So I went down to see him – it was a free meal,

basically. It was a horrible attitude to have, but that's what I felt, so I went along, and he was very nice – telling me that he could make me into a big star. But I'd looked around me, and I'd seen Steve Strange, I'd seen all these people who had really, I thought, played it the wrong way – and I thought that if I'd done it on my own it would only be viewed as very icy, and very kind of amateur . . . . I mean, I could have been very easy – I was offered a lot of money – but I thought, "No, this isn't right. I'll get a band together and I'll play." '

None of George's friends or family could believe he turned down EMI's offer. He was still basically broke, and he did *want* to sing. But there'd already been so much gossip and press about his sexuality and clothes that he couldn't stand the idea of being just another weirdo trendy. He honestly did want to make good music – but moreover, he didn't like the idea of doing something – anything – all on his own. He wanted a band to work with, hang out with, feed ideas to. A sort of surrogate family. He set about finding a band. But he didn't really know where to look. He also didn't know how to play anything. Or how to write songs. Or melodies. But he didn't stop to think about any of those things.

One night in a club, a fellow walked up to George

and said, 'I've seen your picture in the *NME* [*New Musical Express*]. I wanna be in a band with you.' George thought this very nervy, but liked his attitude. 'Oh, simple as that?' he asked. The stranger replied, 'Yeah, I'm a bass player – my name's Mikey Craig.'

George liked him, even if he didn't know if Mikey really could play bass. But it was a beginning, and Mikey *really* wanted to be in a band. George liked that he'd heard of him, had pursued him. So he consented to play with Mikey.

Mikey, like George, grew up just a bit out of central London, in a place called Hammersmith. He was born on February 15, 1960; his father was a singer from Jamaica who'd moved to England, and his mother was also born in Jamaica. Mikey had a traditional English upbringing, with his four sisters and two brothers, except for one thing – he was black.

The white kids at school weren't particularly nice to him, and he didn't seem to care about the things they cared about – like sports and music. Around the age of thirteen, the precocious Mikey started going to the London clubs and convincing the doormen he was eighteen. He didn't care about hanging out, but he *did* care about dancing and hearing the good new records. Later on, he became a DJ himself and taught himself how to play a friend's bass guitar. He picked it up pretty naturally, and liked to imitate a reggae bass line.

At around sixteen, Mikey met Cleo Pizzey, and she became his first girlfriend. They had two kids almost right away, Kito and Amber. He had a number of jobs – roadbuilding, running a sound studio – but he didn't like any of them. He and Cleo were running out of money, so he decided he *had* to join a band. He read all the music papers for months until he noticed a photo of George and Annabella, with a caption that said Malcolm McLaren was starting a new band around this guy named George. Mikey thought George looked so ostentatious, a band with him just might click. One night in a club, he saw George and introduced himself to him.

Well, one down. George had a bass player. Now he needed to find a drummer. A friend of his gave him the phone number of a guy named Jon Moss. George recognized the name and had seen him a few times; Moss had played with punk bands like The Clash and The Damned, and he hung out with the punk crowd on the King's Road. George thought, Oh, no, not a punker – and he and Mikey decided to rehearse without a drummer for a while.

They asked Suede (of Kirk's old band) to play

guitar with them, and called themselves the Sex Gang Children (sex being a popular theme for bands at the time; the name was later passed on to another punk band), but didn't take themselves too seriously. They did write one song called 'Mask' – which George now swears was awful. They really did need a drummer, so George took Kirk's advice and rang up this Jon Moss. All drummers are obnoxious, he thought at the time – so it didn't much matter what the guy was like, as long as he could play.

Jon and George's first meeting was in March of 1981, about a week after George called him. It didn't look too good from the beginning, and was about as likely that they'd hit it off as apples and oranges – or punks and New Romantics. Jon was sick of posers, Blitzers, New Romantics – he just wanted to be in a successful group. He was from a well-to-do family and was an accomplished drummer at this point – he really thought it about time he made something of himself. George, on the other hand, although not really tied in with Steve Strange or the Spandau kids, was featured in every single magazine article on Blitz kids (the crowd that hung out at the Blitz) or New Romantics.

George recalls that first meeting.

'So I called Mikey and Jon down to this rehearsal. Jon walks in – it's so funny – with these really tight jeans on; he looked like a real *lad*, and I thought, God, this isn't gonna work! and he said, "Well, what d'you want me to do?" So I said, "I don't know," and he said, "Well, I'm telling you that I want to start a band." I said, "I agree – I don't want you to come and play drums *for* me. I want you to start a band *with* me." He said, "Okay. That's what I want." Then I said, "Well, great – but I don't know what I want to play, and I don't care, but I want a *set* idea." '

This is Jon's recollection of that fateful meeting:

'I just said, "Hello," and I looked at him. He was very down-to-earth, just said, "Hello – all right?" You know what he's like, sort of flirty, coy. I thought, Oh, he's nice . . . I brought my drums with me and started playing. They had this song called "Mask," which was horrible. Anyway, I remember thinking, This guy is great – George is like that. Everybody likes him. He can be really nasty, he's got a very sharp tongue, but on the whole, he's very lovable . . . I played an African beat, and he said, "Yeah, I like that." So I thought, Great, I can have input, and be creative – this is what I want.'

Jon was born on September 11, 1957, to a young London Jewish girl who couldn't afford to bring him up, so she had him adopted by the Moss family of London, who were also Jewish. Lionel and Aubrey Moss named him Jonathan Aubrey. Lionel worked in the clothing business, and made enough money to give the boy a lovely British middle-class upbringing.

Jon was sent to Church of England schools – because they were the best ones at the time – and he had a tough time with that. His father gave him boxing lessons, starting at the age of five. From that point on, Jon became very active in sports. He was also good in the arts and, particularly, music. He got into it by listening to the radio and then trying to re-create the tunes on his parents' piano. However, Jon didn't start rebelling when he became a teenager – he did well in school, loved his parents, and started playing his brother's drum set after school.

When Jon finished school, his father wanted him to work in a big clothing store with him. But he didn't enjoy that, and took a job at a recording studio – even though he had no idea what to do in one. After that short stint, he had numerous jobs, even selling cakes on the street. He wasn't having any luck in the working world, so he thought he might as well join a band. He started several different ones with friends – Phone Bone, Pastrami Barmy, and Eskimo Norbert, none of which lasted more than a few months. However, he was becoming a pretty competent drummer.

When punk broke out in the late seventies, opportunity knocked. Jon hated punk at first, but he learned to love it. He auditioned for a band that turned out to be The Clash, who were already pretty big. He joined them, but wound up quitting after a few months because he didn't get along with Mick Jones and Joe Strummer. Next he started a new group called London. They immediately got a record deal and went on a tour (those were the days when that was still possible). But after a while without hits, they broke up too.

Next Jon became the drummer with established punk group The Damned. He really liked that – until he got into a car crash and had to quit that group too. He started yet another band, but nothing seemed to be working out at all. He was getting seriously depressed, until a big offer came in: 'Jon, are you working? Adam Ant needs a drummer.' Off he went, to tour with Adam – but he didn't like the music and left. (Six months later, Adam had a huge hit with 'Ant Music.') Then Jon met a musician named Kirk Brandon, who told him that his friend, George O'Dowd, was starting a band – and said he'd give George his number.

* * *

The first thing Jon did in the new band (as yet unnamed) was to fire Suede. 'He isn't any good,' he told George. 'He's a great guy, but he isn't going anywhere – he's a three-chord wonder.' George had known Suede for a long time, had hung out with him. 'I can't sack him!' he wailed to Jon. Jon replied, 'Okay – *I'll* sack him, then.' Surprisingly, Suede took it pretty well: he knew it wasn't working out.

The three – George, Mikey, and Jon – began the search for a new guitarist. They heard lots of people, got sick of it, just wanted to get it over with. They were going to hear one last person, but whoever it was didn't show up. (Bet he's kicking himself now.) George had already auditioned a young guy named Roy Hay, whom he liked – Roy didn't know who George was, didn't know who Mikey was, didn't know who Jon was – and didn't care. He just wanted to play guitar and tried really hard to play what he thought George wanted.

George wanted to hire him – he seemed so nice and unaffected. He said to Jon, 'Let's keep *him*.' Jon wasn't thrilled about the idea, but eventually he agreed.

Roy Hay grew up just outside of London, in Corringham, Essex. He was born Roy Ernest Hay on August 12, 1961, and was a well-behaved youngster who excelled in school and particularly in music. His father got him to take piano lessons as soon as that was apparent.

Roy's older brother was a rock fan, so Roy got to listen to Genesis, Led Zeppelin, and all the great bands in the early seventies. Then his father bought him a guitar and he copied the licks from all the popular songs. He'd get together with all the guys at school, and see who could play them the loudest.

Roy finished school at age sixteen (which is when you finish in England, if you're not going on to college), and had no idea of what he wanted to do at all. So he got a boring job – working in an insurance office in London. He hated it, but unlike Jon or Mikey or even George, he didn't quit – he kept it for three years and practised guitar at home. At nineteen, he'd had it with office life and decided to learn how to cut hair – which he seemed to have a natural flair for.

He kept on playing music at home, mostly for the fun of it. In the summer of 1981, Roy met a girl named Alison Green at a nightclub outside of London and started to go out with her. (He's now married to her.) Then he became the guitarist in her brother's band, called Russian Bouquet. Not long after joining up with them, a friend told him he heard that this fellow George O'Dowd was starting a new band and that he ought to audition. He did – mostly for the hell of it. Roy had never heard of George O'Dowd. He didn't dress up, didn't go to the London clubs – he just wanted to play guitar and not have a horrible job. And that's the very thing that George liked about him when he hired him.

So there they were, a four-piece band. It wasn't a bad combination either. Roy was good at melodies and could write guitar parts. Mikey liked to work on song arrangements and added a reggae/calypso element in the bass line. George couldn't play a thing, but he had lots of ideas for songs – and when he'd get one, he'd just sing it to Roy, who could figure it out. Jon was a great drummer, but he also had something not one of the other members of this new conglomerate had – a real business sense. He seemed to know how to get a band off the ground. George was really impressed.

The first thing Jon wanted to do, right off, was change the band's name. It was still tentatively Sex Gang Children. Jon said, 'No way, man. I'm not interested in the Blitz kids thing, and neither is anyone else anymore. Everything's bleak and cold. *We* need religion – we need warmth – we need *colour*.'

That's just what they got.

5

MAD ABOUT THE BOY

While London was arage with club culture – with bands with oppressive names, and songs with surreal lyrics, while bands performed in black robes and giant crucifixes, while punk still lived in a large part of the population, while England's economy took a nose dive, while unemployment peaked, while everything looked really grim and most successful bands were commercializing on the 'no future' aesthetic – George and Jon were trying to figure out where they stood.

It was in a dingy rehearsal studio in London that Jon talked George out of their adopting the name Sex Gang Children. George, who was now into his semi-Jamaican look and was just starting a line of 'religious'-oriented clothes, stopped to think. He didn't really want to have to pretend he was bizarre anymore. Underneath the clothes, he was more than a bit tired of the pretence of the Blitz club scene, but given how he looked (increasingly more effeminate), he didn't think he'd be accepted anywhere else. He'd spent all his time from age fourteen trying to live up to his own outfits and flamboyance; now it would be interesting to start to convince people he was just like them. Also, his voice was all wrong for the weird stuff – he was good at straight soul vocals, and he was getting better at them all the time.

Jon went on: 'I've been in loads of bands, and now I want to be in a *commercial* band. I want to be in a band that sells loads of records and that your mother likes. I want my mother to like the music I'm making, and I want my baby sister to like it. *I don't care about my friends*; I don't care about the eighteen- to twenty-one-year-old kids, because all *you're* doing is living for other people all the time.'

George, naturally, exploded over this. But his explosion stemmed from some knowledge that this was mostly true. He was just as sick of the 'posey' (dressed-up) bands like Spandau as anyone. But he wasn't sure he was ready, in fact, to be a big star and get written about and be interviewed – and be important outside of the club milieu.

He also wasn't sure he was ready to leave such serious decision-making to Jon Moss – who was a nice bloke and who'd been around the music business, but who just wasn't the kind of person he was used to dealing with. A bit straight, a bit too uncomplicated. Unlike everyone else he knew, Jon didn't seem to be afraid of his temper tantrums.

It was there, in a dingy rehearsal studio in London, that Jon and George dreamed up the name Culture Club – and it seemed to click. First of all, it was a title that allowed them to be *all* things to *all* people, and to borrow from ethnic musics without being called rip-off artists. But it also had the word *club* in the title, referring to George's roots. He couldn't help it, he loved the idea of clubs and gatherings of people. *His* club, however, would be open to everybody – young, old, dressed up, unhip – as long as they liked him. Yes, he wanted *them* to join a club *he* was a member of. And he *liked* the idea of being really the very first member.

It was the autumn of 1981. There was a lot going on, but suddenly George didn't care. He finally had a band, it had a name, and it was all that seemed important. The group wrote some songs almost right away – 'The Eyes of Medusa' and 'I'm an Animal,' and George phoned up the same person at EMI Records who wanted to book him as a solo artist and told him about the songs. Somehow or other, Jon, a good talker on the business end, wrangled studio time out of EMI. They recorded the two songs, but EMI was not impressed at all.

This depressed George, but not Jon. In fact, it only made him more adamant about getting it right. One night before Roy had officially joined the band, Jon told off Suede (the guitarist prior to Roy) in a drunken stupor, as recounted in *When Cameras Go Crazy*, and fired him. He didn't realize he'd already fired him once before.

Jon decided what they needed was rehearsal time. It seemed like a good idea. After all, other bands rehearsed. The only problem was they had to earn money right away. Jon's parents could afford to float him for a bit (they were glad that he wasn't lying around their house anymore), and George had a talent for living on little or no money – his friends fed him and lent him money or gave him odd jobs. But Roy was in big trouble. He was living on the edge of London in Essex with his girlfriend (now wife) Alison, and still working as a hairdresser. He'd work all day, then catch a train, travel for an hour, rehearse from early evening till late, and get home so late he'd feel awful the next day at work. He now says he doesn't know *how* he did it, but that he thought that, if anything, it was his one chance to really be a guitar player.

Mikey was living in his mother-in-law's house,

according to *Cameras*, with his wife and kids. He hated being virtually supported by his relatives and had a real conflict, being a father and trying to be in a rock band – but he didn't know what else to do.

After rehearsing for a few months, George began to think more consistently about the songs he was writing, or trying to write. When Roy began to help with the writing, things came together a bit more. He remembers, 'George and I wrote a song called "Put It Down" in his flat. He has always really been into lyrics – he sang this lyric, and I played around a bit. It was all very vague until we got a drumbeat. Then we put vocals on top.' They got into some writing habits and started writing a whole bunch of songs, the whole group kicking in ideas and riffs.

George was remembering what Jon had said about the 'warm' image – and thinking about the Third World undertones of the music and how that might go with a visual image. George got Sue Clowes to help him flesh out his ideas, and they came up with giant smocks and T-shirts with religious symbols – crosses and Hebrew and Arabic letters – on them. Some people thought the designs sacrilegious, but that spurred George on all the more. George and Sue called it the Foundry Look when the underground fashion magazines asked about it – and said that it was a reaction against the 'pretence of New Romanticism.' It was a sexless and ageless look, and totally afashionable. And the only place anyone could get it was at George and Sue's shop, the Foundry.

It helped Culture Club get some attention in 1981. (Later on, it helped in a big way.) The band's name got mentioned a bit in the music press, and they decided to try playing live, at a New Romantic club called Crocs in Roy's hometown in Essex.

It was a Saturday night in October 1981, and all the kids, average age around seventeen, were drinking and wanting to get crazy. The Culture Club of 1981 was a lot crazier than the Culture Club of 1984. There was no harmonica, no horns, no piano, no backup vocalists – just loud guitars and drums, and George. Jon cranked up the sound, and the band could have been any punk band – or any band at all. The kids danced like crazy (they were not a London crowd) and screamed for more. 'We played most of the first album then,' says Mikey, 'though obviously in different form.'

This was encouraging, gave them something to hope for. Maybe, if they were no good at recording, they'd get to be a really good live band. Culture Club played another gig at Crocs about three

(Photo © Deborah Feingold)

Left to right: Roy Hay, Jon Moss, Mikey Craig, Boy George.
(Photo © Deborah Feingold)

Boy's tropical look.
(Photo by Mark Le Bon/Retna Ltd.)

Culture Club's first American tour.
(*Photo © Ebet Roberts*)

Clowning around in New York. *(Photo © Ebet Roberts)*

Boy George in his early Foundry look.
(Photo © Laura Levine)

Roy Hay sports dreadlocks late in 1983. *(Photo by Dave Hogan/LGI © 1984)*

Boy George and former friend Marilyn.
(Photo by Frank Spooner/Gamma Agency)

Guitar player Roy Hay. (Photo by Anastasia Pantsios/Star File)

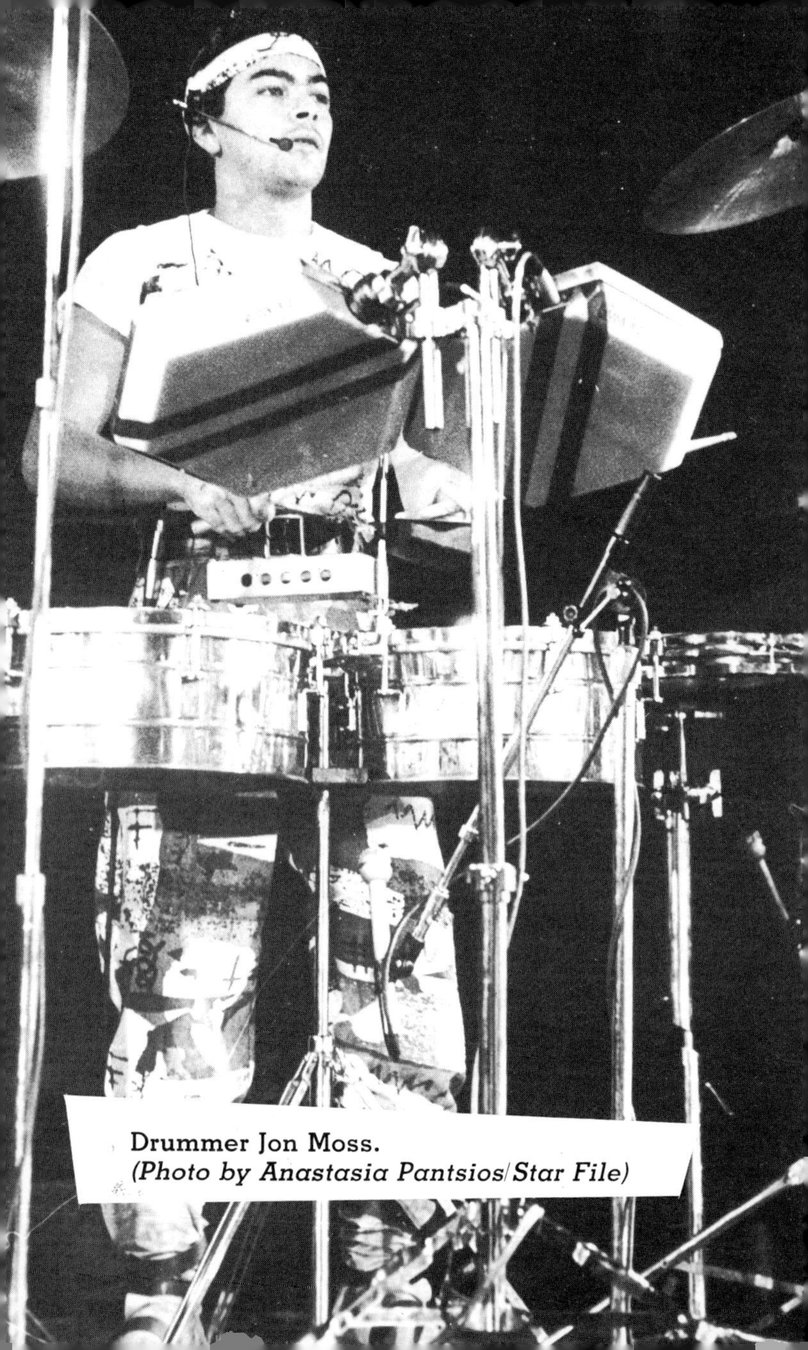

Drummer Jon Moss.
(Photo by Anastasia Pantsios/Star File)

Bass player Mikey Craig.

(Photo by Anastasia Pantsios/Star File)

Returning to England with gifts from fans.
(Wide World Photos)

Boy George's mum, Diana, gets into the Boy-look.
(Photo © Brian Moody/Colorific/Wheeler Pictures)

Boy and Joan Rivers dish dirt over tea.
(Photo by Richard Young/Retna Ltd.)

Singer Helen Terry with Boy George.
(Photo © Michael Putland/Retna Ltd.)

Boy George and his friend Miko
at Nice Airport.
(Photo by Dave Hogan/LGI © 1984)

months later – and it was the luckiest night of their career.

'I want to have a meeting with whoever your manager is,' the young man was saying. Standing in his shop, the Foundry, George wasn't sure he was hearing correctly.

'I want the rights to the publishing of your music,' the young man went on.

'You're not *serious*, are you?' asked George incredulously. 'Come *off* it, we're *useless.*'

'Well,' the young man replied, 'I am serious. I think you're really good.'

The young man knew what he was talking about. He was Danny Goodwin of Virgin Records, an independent label known for signing the best new acts in England, such as Heaven 17 and UB40. He'd seen their second show at Crocs in Essex and was very excited about it.

'I was *always* very pessimistic in those days,' says George now. 'Jon was definitely the backbone of Culture Club in those days. I was always saying to him, "We should give up," and he'd say, "No – you're a really good singer" – but I never used to think I was, and when we recorded demos, they were so *awful* – I was embarrassed about them. I played the demos for my parents, and some of my relatives went, "Uh . . ." You could tell they thought it was a pile of crap.

'Myself and Mikey were very lazy then – although Mikey wouldn't admit that. But I *know* we were a pile of slobs. Jon would say, "I don't want to mess about, I'm not taking this crap." And Roy was real serious about the music itself.' George would have given up after the gigs if it hadn't been for Jon. Jon was dying to get a chance to do more demos. George was afraid to. Danny Goodwin got Virgin to back another set of demos.

But after they cut the demos (with songs on it that have never been released, like 'Put It Down,' 'I'm Not Crazy,' and 'Kissing to Be Clever'), Virgin moved over to George's way of thinking. The demos weren't great. They weren't horrible either – but something was definitely missing. It was in George's voice – there just wasn't any real *conviction.* He was sounding like Smokey Robinson, he was sounding like Gladys Knight (one of his favourite singers), but it wasn't coming off.

'Then it just clicked one day,' George recalls. 'I said, "I want to sound like *me.*" ' So it was back to the drawing board and more demos. This time they convinced EMI Records, who were still somewhat interested, to give them a studio to work in. They were working on the song called 'The Eyes of Medusa' when an EMI engineer *stopped* the recording session.

'Excuse me,' he said to George, 'you're singing about a *guy*.'

George answered, 'Yeah.'

The engineer repeated, 'You're singing about a *man*?'

George repeated, 'Yeah.'

'Well, you're not allowed to do that.'

George replied flatly, as if to his teachers at school, 'I'm allowed to do what I like.'

And the engineer answered, ' . . . Okay.'

George claims in retrospect that the song was not about sex at all, but about a male Medusa. 'But eventually we got it done, and Jon went on holiday to America and took this tape to some of his nouveau riche relatives in L.A., and they said, "Oh, my God!" ' That's pretty much what EMI said, also.

'I think a lot of bands are frightened about credibility, whereas I've never really seen us as *musicians*,' recounts George. 'The band, really, has been a series of accidents from beginning to end.'

EMI *was*, however, intereted in some of Culture Club's demos, but Culture Club was not interested in them. 'They couldn't see me in any kind of future whatsoever,' says George. And both he and Jon, anxious as they were to sign a deal, if only for the sake of getting money to rehearse with, hated the idea of giant record companies. George felt the personnel at the big record companies would never like him as a person; that they simply wanted to cash in on his odd looks and newspaper stardom. As much as he wanted attention, George had seen too many freaky-looking friends turn into flashes-in-the-pan when their look went out of style.

Danny Goodwin was still interested in Culture Club, though. He just had a hunch – he saw the way the kids went crazy for them at Crocs. Their newest demos, done at EMI, had some promise, and they had Tony Gordon, a familiar London music-biz person, advising and helping them.

And Culture Club was still interested in Virgin Records. Why? 'They all shout at each other there,' says Jon. 'It's like chaos – but it's cash from chaos, and it really works. If we were ever going to make it, we'd make it like they made it.' Or, as Jon also says, 'We were offered better deals on paper – but I'd rather have seventy-five percent of a million, than a hundred percent [of] nothing.'

'What are you going to do with your band?' Virgin Records asked Jon and George. 'Are you going to play little clubs? Are you going to play secret gigs? Are you going to get your friends working for you?'

'No.'

'What will you do then?'

'Tours. We'll do tours.'

Virgin was a bit surprised to hear Jon Moss say that, but they weren't going to argue with him; he seemed so resolute. They'd broken most of their pop acts (again, Heaven 17 and UB40) in the London club circuit, and they were sure this band would get its big push that way too. That was one of the reasons they'd signed Culture Club – everyone in that scene was waiting to see George succeed or flop right on his made-up nose. Malcolm McLaren had started the technique of the 'secret gig' – where a band played unannounced, but all the 'right' people were informed. Everyone in London wanted to be 'the right people' so badly, they'd *love* the band.

Jon's idea of a 'short tour' was to hit the universities. The student audiences they played to very often were drinking beer and would have welcomed anything. They did seem to like the songs, though – which were rough versions of the songs on *Kissing to Be Clever*. Just once, in Glasgow, Scotland (a notoriously rough town for bands, or *anything*, for that matter), the audience was hostile. Sure enough, that night George lost his voice (which was otherwise improving steadily) for the first time and had to leave the stage. There wasn't much the band could do without him, so they departed as well. But, more important, the London gigs went over pretty well.

George had this great idea. The band had released, on Virgin, two of their songs – 'White Boy' and 'I'm Afraid of Me.' The second one got some play in the London clubs, but neither made the charts. George's idea was to bring in guest musicians and make each song sound really unique. Surprise people. He wanted the third single to be a song he'd written called 'Do You Really Want to Hurt Me,' and he wanted to get a 'toaster' (a person who can rap in Jamaican patois) to talk over the instrumental part. Someone suggested a girl named Helen Terry to do some backup singing on it. And Tony Gordon, now the band's manager, suggested a young recording engineer named Steve Levine to handle producing.

Jon and George wanted to put this single out fast, quick, before the band faded into oblivion. They'd already recorded the first album in bits and pieces, but Jon knew it would go nowhere unless they had a single that made the charts. Virgin consented to release another single.

George had the idea to make 'Do You Really Want to Hurt Me' a bit reggaeish, and Steve Levine was behind it. When they went into the studio, nobody was really in agreement as to what they wanted. George liked *that* idea too – he thought. Why shouldn't we *all* do what we think is best on this song?

Within a few weeks of its release, 'Do You Really Want to Hurt Me' was the number one song in England. Nobody really knows how it happened, except that its soft reggae sound was different from any music coming out of London, and that its lyrics were surprisingly vulnerable, and seemingly sincere. It's also important to note that when the single went to number one, most of the record-buying public in England did not know who Boy George was, nor did they know what he looked like. Nor did they care. Until they found out.

Within about six weeks, 'Do You Really Want to Hurt Me' was number one all over Europe. Nobody wanted to hurt George – yet.

Here are some of the first reviews Culture Club ever received in the British music press on 'Do You

Really Want to Hurt Me.' *New Musical Express*'s reviewer claimed Culture Club astounded him, because they were quite talented on top of their trendiness. He demanded 'Do You Really Want to Hurt Me' become a hit. The *Melody Maker*'s reviewer asked how anyone would want to 'hurt Boy George?' The reviewer called him refreshingly emotional, and said he wasn't at all the poser he was cracked up to be.

Things weren't as rosy as they seemed. Jon was happy; he had what he wanted. George was a bit confused. But right before the big success, Mikey's wife, Cleo, took their two kids and left for New Mexico with her mother. Mikey tried to keep them from going, but he knew he was just on the verge and couldn't let success elude him.

Roy took the opportunity of the band's first success to marry his girlfriend, Alison. They tied the knot on Christmas Eve, 1982. Good thing too. He hasn't had a day off since.

But meanwhile, all hell began to break loose. George's picture, naturally, began to appear in the press, with headlines in the British dailies like 'IS IT A HER? A HIM? – OR IS IT NEITHER?' 'CHART-BUSTING SINGER HAS PLUNGED ROCK WORLD INTO CONFUSION!' 'I DON'T CARE IF PEOPLE THINK I'M A GIRL, SAYS BOY GEORGE.' 'HE IS NUMBER

ONE ON THE CHARTS, AND THEY CALL HIM A GENDER BENDER.' 'WOULD YOU WANT TO SLEEP WITH A BOY LIKE THIS?'

The British press *loves* a good scandal. If there isn't one in Parliament, they'll find one elsewhere. The scandal created by the press over the Sex Pistols in the late 1970s was what brought that group its success. Was George equally lucky, or unlucky? Surprisingly, this sort of nasty press didn't hurt him as much as it could have. After all, he had a number-one record. Virgin was telling him he could really 'do it' now. He'd been called names since he was fourteen; he was pretty used to it. His parents and family didn't like the negative attention at all, but they were proud of him – he'd done it on his own, and he'd *finally* made something of himself – and his outrageous clothes.

The press, as usual, threw in their two cents (or pence, as is the case in England). 'The most outrageous character since Elton John and Liberace,' raved the *Daily Express*. 'Wally of the Week,' screamed *Sunday People Magazine*. That's a very dubious award, given to the person who's the silliest at that moment in the eyes of the press.

George had a couple of equally good replies in print – even at the time of the band's early success, he gave great interviews, seemed completely unharried by even the most personal questions (which were mostly all he was asked – no one asked about the music then), and made his quotes *so* quotable, the press didn't *dare* not print them. Yes, Boy George was great copy.

In the early days, the press was clearly more interested in Boy George's sexual habits than in the band's musical accomplishments. And while the Boy admitted in *NME* that he was just a 'bloke with a bit of an ego problem,' he pretty well managed to dance around a direct answer to their intensely personal questions.

Answers ranged from: 'Sex is not an obsession with me. It's like eating a bag of crisps – quite nice, but nothing marvellous' to 'Oh, I've slept with girls and blokes, but I'm not sleeping with anybody right now – can't be bothered to work up the energy to find someone.' George, who started calling himself 'Boy George' at this time because so many people thought he was a girl, even went so far as to say, 'I'm *not* a poof. I'm effeminate in the way I look, but I'm not an effeminate person.'

His most definitive (of sorts) quote on his sexuality was printed in an interview in *New Musical Express*.

'I don't think that I could now sleep with anyone unless I loved them . . . I'm not sexy in a physical way. I'm not physically attractive, I don't wish to be. If I was, I would certainly cover it up, because I think there's certain things you've got to leave to your imagination. I mean, I wouldn't take a girl out in a miniskirt, with her bra showing. I just think that's horrible. Most people would rather go to bed with a teddy bear than someone overwhelmingly sexy. I just don't find perfection attractive at all.'

6

COVER BOY

By the end of 1982, Boy George was as recognizable a 'cover girl' as Brooke Shields. His beautifully painted face graced the covers of big British publications like *The Face, Chart-busters, Smash Hits, New Musical Express*, and *Record Mirror*. But he also turned up, in varying styles of regalia, in European magazines such as *Salut!* from France, *Popcorn* from Germany, *Pop Rocky* from Holland, as well as in Japanese, Israeli, and continental fashion magazines. Yet it still wasn't his music that was making George an international celebrity. It was his willingness to confuse the issue of his sexuality and the fact that he hid *nothing*. Although he was becoming notorious and, therefore, an open target for mockery, George was growing increasingly positive about himself. The press was very much surprised to find that he was virtually undaunted.

Said Jon Moss about that time, in a *Melody Maker* interview: 'The only thing I worry about is that George is gonna get upset. I feel sorry for him – he's very emotional.' Jon went on to say that he was always having to convince George that the stuff in the press was nonsense, but that George took the press's admonitions pretty seriously at first. 'I don't think, no matter what they've written, that George has *ever* done anything that he's really ashamed of – and as long as you take that attitude, it doesn't matter what's written. The amazing thing about George is that, in the end, he makes all those people look stupid, he's proved all those people who said we were just a bunch of dressed-up floosies wrong.'

Mikey Craig also had strong feelings about George and his press attention. He recounted them in the same issue of *Melody Maker:* 'The bloody media doesn't help things at *all*. They don't understand a bloody thing, they really don't. Sometimes you could cry when you look at the things they write, and George doesn't help, because he allows the media to carry on as they are. I mean, if George was really on the case, he'd sometimes stop certain things happening, but he *enjoys* it. He needs a hell of a lot of attention – I think that's probably why he just lets it run along, because if he *didn't* get that attention, he would probably feel lost and insecure. The dangerous thing is that there was a time when he *believed* the press, when he believed all the crap in the papers – Boy George, front pages, blah, blah, blah – and he was rising to it – but he's cooled down a lot more now. He doesn't like to admit he's wrong, *ever*! He would *never* admit it. I felt sorry for him, really, because it could happen to anybody – your face is in the paper every day, and you suddenly go off on a trip. The press has made Culture Club more *George* than anything, and kind of rifted us for time – us, *and* him.'

George's response to his fast (like *lightning*) press stardom was characteristically outspoken and commonsensical: 'Some rock musicians are so uninterested in being anything special, they're *so* interested in music, they don't *want* to be a personality. But I've really cultivated this whole idea of being a personality; I've really *wanted* to be one, *because* I'm aware I'm a good musician. I'm aware that I can sing and write good songs, so I don't have to keep on going on about *that.*'

In Britain and on the Continent, Culture Club released two other singles off the *Kissing to Be Clever* album: 'Time (Clock of the Heart)' and 'I'll Tumble 4 Ya.' They were quite different from 'Do You Really Want to Hurt Me' in that they were uptempo positive-attitude love songs, with a lot of Motown-nostalgia feeling. George's personality wasn't at all the subject of these lyrics, as in 'Do You Really Want to Hurt Me,' and his voice was getting smoother and sweeter. 'British soul' was a movement that had been brewing for a while (as a reaction to New Romanticism, which, by 1982, *everybody* had exhausted), but Culture Club's was the most mellow, the least synthesized, and most *emotional* – especially the lyrics. At this point, attention was focused on everything *but* George's songwriting capabilities. Nevertheless, that talent was revealing itself as he became more confident. Both of the singles went to number one all over Europe.

After it was released in the U.S., *Kissing to Be Clever* sold over three million copies worldwide – highly successful, for a debut album. What, after all, did 'it' for the band? A band's image doesn't sell millions of records. Neither does its press coverage. In the end, it was the songs that did it for Culture Club – though nobody but George realized that for a long time. Each individual song on the album was different, each was melodic, rhythmic, its own little world.

'Do You Really Want to Hurt Me' (which has gone on to sell seven million copies as a single) was almost not the band's first choice for their third single (and meant-to-be first hit). '*Nobody* wanted this song,' Jon recalled later. 'Not even Virgin wanted it – although Simon Draper of Virgin says *he* did. But one day, I heard it, and I thought, "Blimey, if I could remix that, that song's gonne be a *monster*." I just *heard* it, y'know?'

'Time (Clock of the Heart)' showed that Boy George could write pretty semisweet love songs (which would become his forte later on). 'Love is the most important thing in the world,' George says of his penchant for sentimental songs. 'Everyone wants to be needed, and everyone wants to be loved. Love songs are the one thing that everyone can relate to – that's why most of my songs are love songs.'

'I'm Afraid of Me' – the first single – was a song that was underestimated. It's got a calypso beat and melody, with steel drum playing on it, with a bizarre, almost paranoid lyric – 'I'm afraid of *me* . . . ?' People weren't sure they were hearing it right. George will only explain this song by saying, 'I write about the politics of people. I don't write about the politics of Margaret Thatcher or Ronald Reagan. I write about the things that affect me, the way people behave around me. There are certain people that I could tell you the songs are about, but

I don't want to make them heroes in my songs.'

'White Boy' was another single that failed to take off, although it was played in clubs. Some people thought it racist and couldn't understand what this band with a black bass player, Jewish drummer, and Jamaican backup singers were doing with a racist song. George has always defended it this way: 'It's *not* about white people, it's about people who are shallow, see-through. Also, at the time I started, there were a lot of cynical people around me, saying, "Oh, your band's really *white*, you should be tribal." I just kept saying, "We're a rock band, we're going to do all the things that people who've come out of clubs don't do." '

Culture Club's music wasn't the only thing catching on all over Europe and Japan. The Foundry clothes – or, at least, the look (as George describes it, 'street tramp or hobo') – was spreading like wildfire. It was the first new and original rock 'n' roll look to come out of Britain for some time that kids found accessible, fun, and flattering to everyone. The word is that every little fat girl in Britain was forever grateful to Boy George for giving her enough fabric to hide her girlish pulchritude. Boys were glad to be able to wear big bright printed clothes and not have to get into arguments, defending their taste. But even beyond the clothes, the hats and scarves caught on too. Kids were buying fake dreadlocks to pin onto their hair.

After their first big singles, George pulled himself out of the London club scene (he was now too conspicuous to go and have fun), but it was hardly finished with *him*. The clubs were now packed with kids in the 'Boy George' look, and so many Boy George clones began turning up everywhere (as is documented in the Culture Club video 'Church of the Poison Mind') that their photos started turning up as often as George's. The club's most famous Boy might have extricated himself from his roots, but he still reigned as 'King of Clubs' – and really still does, since he put that scene on the map more than anyone.

American fashion designer Betsey Johnson, who was the first U.S. designer to make high fashion out of street clothes in the sixties, paid homage to George's fashion sense: 'It's always nice when someone comes along and picks up the fashion industry. He's an inspiration to wear what you want, how you want it. I have a sweater in my line named the "Boy George sweater," and people love it. It's a big, loose shape, and it's a very boy-girl unsexy thing . . . when I think of Boy George, I think of big shapes.'

* * *

George may have been Europe's Boy, but over in the not-very-trendy U.S.A., only a handful of people with good ears and a sharp eye for style picked up on Culture Club. George knew he was going to have to virtually start all over again to make anything of the band in the U.S. He was warned that America would never take to him or his image, that he'd get much less press coverage than he'd ever received in Britain.

Culture Club's American licensing of their records went to Epic Records, a division of CBS, widely thought to be the most powerful record company in America and in the world. Epic is also the label that spawned Michael Jackson's solo success and the recent superstardom of Cyndi Lauper. It's also the label that helped Quiet Riot sell millions of albums in just a few months. Epic was behind Culture Club, was sure they could sell the singles in the U.S. Sure enough, by the winter of 1983 'Do You Really Want to Hurt Me' went all the way in the *Billboard* charts to the number-two record in the country. Culture Club *had* to do a few dates in the U.S. to support the release of their first album. George *hated* flying, and he was pretty nervous about American audiences, who were known for under-reaction – at least, compared to British ones. Still, he agreed – Culture Club had to play America. In December of 1982, they consented to cross the Atlantic – like Columbus, not knowing at all what they'd find.

'What a drag. I'm talking about Boy George. You'd think anyone who goes to the trouble of adopting the quirkiest pop identity since Tiny Tim would at least exhibit a little personality on stage.'

Robert Hilburn, music editor of the *Los Angeles Times*, was not altogether enthusiastic about the first Culture Club concert he saw and reviewed. 'But there was no hint of charisma as he simply moved about the Hollywood Palladium stage over the weekend, going through a few clumsy dance steps and some awkward bunny hops. So, we're looking at another case of a quick-to-rise, quick-to-fade, rock attraction from England, right? Don't bet on it. Boy George and his band, Culture Club, have an ace up their sleeve. He's a clever songwriter, and he's got one of the sweetest, most soulful voices of any young singer in years. And his band has a great feel for mixing reggae, pop, and Latin rhythms to spicy dance numbers. In other words, there's irony at work here. In a field where image is all that some acts have going for them, the image-conscious Boy George is blessed with a rather old-fashioned virtue: talent.'

Hilburn went on to note that if Boy George could get the audience past his peculiar ensembles, his songs could have real universality.

Of course, Hilburn didn't realize his prophecy would come true – his review epitomized America's first look at Boy George: He's weird, he's a bit stiff onstage, but he's got feelings, and he's got a voice.

Stephen Holden reviewed Culture Club's first U.S. show at The Ritz in New York City in December of 1982 in *The New York Times*. He noted how George 'managed thoroughly to obscure conventional distinctions of both sex *and* ethnicity . . . . Singing in a voice that suggests a cross between Smokey Robinson and early 1960's teenage idols . . . '

Holden was duly impressed, yes. But the *Village Voice* reviewer was not that impressed: 'Boy George is Britain's current "sex symbol," and the band that's legitimized him is Culture Club . . . they've beguiled the normally intelligent British press for months. George O'Dowd, former London club persona, seems to have done the right homework for the wrongest of reasons: to ensure there'd never be a door policy he couldn't crack. The band's name is so perfect, and so ironic . . . . None of this is played for theatrics in Culture Club's live show, as evidenced last weekend at The Ritz . . . .

Yeah, George can torch, but he's got no fire, he never warms up enough to flirt with the audience . . . . George has captured the look of love, and that's about all.'

Yes, the first show was weak, badly performed. It was difficult to pick the band out from the influx of pop trendies hitting American stages from England. Plus the songs on the first album, except for 'Do You Really Want to Hurt Me' and 'Time,' were still a bit immature.

'Now *who* do you think would want to hurt *me*?' asked a colourfully dressed Boy George of his New York audience at the West Side Pier in the summer of 1983. He might have been referring to his critics, but the kids in the crowd went hysterical at the thought. Hurt Boy George? He was like a big teddy bear.

George was obviously still conscious of his first U.S. gigs and the lukewarm reception they'd received. He'd been criticized for being 'stiff' on-stage in England too – Culture Club's act was often referred to as 'a bit dull,' with not a lot going on.

Well, by 1983 George was feeling a lot more comfortable, just being on a stage in general – which made him more animated. But the real highlight of the summer '83 tour was the new songs. The band had rehearsed all the songs from the upcoming *Colour By Numbers* album and knew how powerful they were. By the end of the rousing show, the entire audience was in love with Boy George. *Hurt* him? They all wanted to take him home! What had really changed was this – Culture Club wasn't afraid of America any more. After all, they'd had three top-ten singles. *Kissing to Be Clever* was the first debut album ever to accomplish that.

Hilburn had been right – radio stations played the music because it was tuneful and pleasant. And it wasn't just kids who craved top-40 hits who were listening to Culture Club. Black and white audiences alike bought *Kissing to Be Clever*, and Culture Club won the same American soul audience that was into Motown and reggae. Their singles made it in pop charts, dance charts, and the black music charts in *Billboard* magazine – meaning that Culture Club songs were getting heavy airplay on urban soul radio stations. Those stations didn't care about trendy English nightclubbers; they just liked the sound: It was smooth, soulful, sweet, and funky.

It was interesting that Culture Club should achieve the success referred to in the music business as a 'crossover act.' Not too many recording artists have been able to pull that off. Culture Club and Michael Jackson are both forerunners of a new movement – white artists who can get on black stations, and black artists who can have major pop and rock hits. Is it just a coincidence that both Culture Club and Michael Jackson are on Epic Records? Epic is known for having the best team of 'promotion men' (hired for their skill at getting records played on the radio) in the business. That's got something to do with it, but not everything. Both Boy George and Michael Jackson did one thing at the right time – they fused rock and soul. They picked up on the tradition that Motown established.

It also didn't hurt Culture Club that they quickly became MTV favourites. Kids might have been surprised by George's appearance, but they couldn't take their eyes off him. MTV ran Culture Club's videos, but they also ran interview footage of the Boy, just being himself (hip, irreverent, disarming). America got to know Boy George a lot more slowly than England did – but after it got to know him, it fell for him fast.

George told an interviewer from *Musician* magazine at the end of the summer 1983 tour, 'I'm constantly being asked if my image fits in with the traditional forms of music we play – will we sell to hamburger queens and truckers all over the West? Yet the way I look at it is very obviously contradictory to that. I think this is very good, I *like* contradictions . . . . It's kind of boring when things are just what they are, don't you think?'

Roy Hay added offhandedly, 'Yeah, George is a great lover of contradictions. That's his thing. I like nice chords, he likes contradictions.'

Indeed, Culture Club uses contradictions all across the board. They employ so many different symbols, in their videos, in their clothes, in their album graphics: gender signs, Stars of David, Oriental calligraphy, crosses. What's it all mean? Is it *meant* to be confusing? Does George *mean* to contradict, with his voice versus looks appeal? His answer is 'I *like* to change people's opinions about me. It's boring preaching to the converted.'

That's how Boy George conquered America. He enjoys being misunderstood by projecting an enigmatic, complicated image. Then he reveals that he's really quite nice and normal, not an outlaw at all.

Jon Moss explains the band's use of symbols in this way. 'We use all sorts of symbols. It's a good way of presenting them without meaning anything specific. Culture Club uses *everything*. Our message is, "Everything is interesting, and you should take what's good about them, but don't take just one symbol and let that represent you." '

If Culture Club's image and style is eclectic, so is their music. This is how their musical roles seem to break down: Jon and Roy have rock backgrounds and add that element to the songs. Mikey's influence is more ethnic – he's into reggae, calypso, and Caribbean sounds. The melodies pretty much originate with George – and, says Mikey, 'A lot of our r & b and contemporary black sounds start with George. He's a white soul singer, basically.'

But here's George's own description of his vocal style: 'I didn't want to be another Bryan Ferry or Bowie. I didn't want to be another great white hope with an angular voice, going "Ooh-woo-woo" in a really affected way. I'm not interested in that crap. They may be good entertainers, but they're not good singers – and being a good singer is really my main thing. I want to be more like Rod Stewart or Marvin Gaye or Smokey Robinson – or even like Sting. All those people have distinctive voices, and they're the people that you remember.'

None of the band, however, really knew how to write songs. They wound up learning together, and now they almost always write together and credit the songs to the whole band. George will come up with a sort-of-melody and sing it to Jon, Roy, and Mikey. Jon will flesh it out with a beat, Roy will start fiddling with arranging a melody, Mikey will try various bass lines, and off they go. However, according to George, 'When we write, we fight. We call each other useless; we tell each other how useless we are – a lot of abuse flies. But at the end of the day, I think we all want the same thing – so we really work well together. Everyone makes the same amount of money, regardless of what they do. When we first got together, the bands played a lot of favourite songs: disco, reggae, Philadelphia soul, hard rock, top-forty pop. Having picked these songs apart, we began to put our own songs together. I think Culture Club is the most honest form of modern plagiarism in music. We just *take* things. Plagiarism is acknowledging the similarity between "Church of the Poison Mind" and – "Baby baby, everthing is alright, uptight." A lot of musicians claim they're very original, which I think is very boring. You're not born with a stock of information, so you are what you pick up. Bowie has always, always, avoided the subject of where he gets his ideas. But I say, "Yes, we take from other people." '

The band also gives credit to their producer, Steve Levine, who's become famous for the Culture Club sound – he's worked with them since the beginning, and he probably won't ever *not* work with them. 'He really taught us technology,' said Mikey. 'He was a big influence at first, because he knew all of the technical aspects, and we were learning. Now, on the new upcoming album, he's more like an ambassador. He directs things in the studio to make sure that people don't clash and things run smoothly.'

After the summer of 1983 tour, the boys went back to Britain to put the finishing touches on *Colour By Numbers*. All in all, they hadn't done too badly in the States – a million and a half albums were sold. Not bad at all. Meanwhile, George was overwhelmed with a new honour – readers of a Swiss music magazine voted him 'the most beautiful person in the world.' His looks were starting to work for him, instead of what was expected. Readers of the London *Sun* voted him 'Face of the Year,' second only to one of his favourites, Princess Diana (she claims George is one of her favourites too).

7

FROM RAGS TO RICH RAGS

You know what they say about recent converts – that they're always the most fanatical. That is what happened to the British public after Culture Club's American success. Suddenly Boy George was 'Our Boy,' a credit to the British record business, a credit to Britishness in general – an all-round great chap. Virgin Records were patting themselves on the back – they'd taken a gamble and come up with gold.

Meanwhile, amazing stories related to Culture Club were popping up on the pages of the British dailies. One sixteen-year-old British girl recently came out of a coma after hearing a taped message made for her by her favourite singer, Boy George of Culture Club. Lisa Greene had been in a coma for three weeks due to a head injury suffered in a car accident. Her parents remembered that Boy

George was her favourite singer and sent a request to his manager, asking him to record a message. Boy George was extremely touched and sent a tape to the hospital. It reportedly started off with Culture Club music and then George's voice, saying 'Please get better, because everyone loves you.' Lisa Greene did wake up and is now *completely* recovered. She's even going to meet her idol – Boy George has invited her to visit the band in the studio.

In October of 1983, Culture Club released *Colour By Numbers*, their second album. No one knew what to expect. It didn't really *matter* what was on it, Britain was prepared to buy it. But America wasn't – American radio only wants hits. 'Church of the Poison Mind' was the first single, and it sounded more like Motown than what fans were used to from Culture Club. Within weeks of its release, 'Church' was one of America's top ten. Boy George found himself the first ambassador of the 'British invasion' of bands – he graced the cover of *Rolling Stone* in November of 1983; the cover story was 'England Swings.'

Rolling Stone's approval signalled something big – putting George as the vanguard of a big movement (the place where everyone in the movement already knew he belonged) and mentioning his name throughout the article – within short interviews with all his friends.

It also recounted one of George's favourite tales of 'mistaken identity,' which happens to him a lot (as you can imagine). It seems one night not too long ago, the Boy and chums got all decked out (even more than usual) and went out to have dinner at Langan's, a well-known London restaurant. A rather drunk patron, a man, heard their conversation and decided to plop down next to them to get a better listen. He took a seat next to George.

He began staring at George, and began liking what he saw. George didn't exclaim when he felt the guy's hand on his knee – he thought it was funny.

But the gentleman kept raising his hand, until he'd gone too far – and discovered what to him was the awful truth. 'You're a bloke!' he cried, and jumped to his feet. George thought this was great and smiled at him sweetly.

'But *I* don't find myself particularly physically attractive,' George told *Rolling Stone*. 'That's why I wear baggy clothes. I *know* what makes me successful: I'm funny. I'm not a very serious person. When we make videos, I want people to laugh at them. I want them to be able to feel affection for this image, you know? 'Cause that whole New Romantic thing was very unaffectionate – that's what I found.'

Yes, George had found his niche as a funny man. America was seeing so much of him by the autumn of 1983, it had figured out how to categorize him: the second coming, pop version, of Liberace. He wasn't preaching to kids to leave home, he had no subversive message. In fact, the Boy specifically posed with Boy Mum (as Diana O'Dowd is now called) for several shootings, to let everybody know that he loves his family and that family life is good. George didn't want to corrupt anyone's daughters, or even their sons – he just wanted everybody to like him.

It was 'Karma Chameleon,' the second single off Culture Club's second album, that did it for them. When Culture Club released the song in England a few months earlier, it became Virgin Records' biggest-selling single *ever*. It was an odd choice for a single, an odd pop tune no matter how you looked at it. It sounds sort of countryish – no hint of reggae or rock in it whatsoever. This is how George described 'Karma' before it was released: 'One of the tracks on the new album is very country-sounding. I want to write songs that apply to everyone. We haven't got a particular sound. It's a big gamble, I know, but I don't want to imitate what we've done before – that's not interesting for us or the audience.'

Even George was surprised at 'Karma's' American success. It went gold and stayed number one for three weeks on *Billboard*'s chart. ' "Karma Chameleon" was something I wrote at school,' he told *Melody Maker* when it went to number one. 'It was really an old tune that I had, which Roy wouldn't work out, because he hated it so much. It was like "Kumbaya" – y'know – and he wouldn't play it. I told him, "It's a *great* song, you'll see." It's one of those songs that you either love or hate immediately. It can really grow on you – it can kind of beat you to surrender.'

The lyrics on songs from the second album were a lot more sophisticated than those on the first. They sometimes seemed a bit obscure, but it was obvious George was developing a personal little lyric mythology of his own, the mark of a sophisticated lyricist. For instance, he borrowed the idea of the 'church of the poison mind' from a book on Japanese culture, which he's very much into. The 'colours' that he refers to in 'Karma Chameleon' – red, gold, and green – are from the Jamaican Rastafarians, people George thinks have a great philosophy. Unfortunately, the rest of the band members were a bit sceptical about the lyrics. Roy even said, 'George tries to explain the songs sometimes, and he makes me laugh, because he sits there, and someone'll say to him, "What does that song about the poison mind mean?" – and I've seen him give five different replies!'

Still, the kids related to the new lyrics – they were very emotional. 'Victims' is a slow, torchy, even schmaltzy song about victims of bad love affairs. George said it was his favourite on the album and wanted to release it as a single. The rest of the group was sure it wouldn't be a hit – it had no dance beat (it has no beat whatsoever – it's basically all piano and horns), and record buyers only buy hits. However, it was released in the U.K. (never in the U.S.) as the album's third single – and although it got virtually no radio airplay, it got to number three on the British charts. 'It was taking a risk, but we don't care about that,' Jon told the English music press. 'We've always released exactly what we wanted to; we've never worried about trying to follow things up. "Victims" is such a beautiful song, a real Christmasy-type song – it just suits that time of year y'know, when it's cold and all warm inside. It's a very romantic song, and we didn't care if it did well.' Whether they cared or not, it did.

The other strong element about the new songs

was their arrangements. They had more melody and more instrumentation (thanks to Steve Levine, who loves the sound of harmonicas and horns). They also had Helen Terry's torchy vocals (she was the girl who sang the doot-de-doots' on Lou Reed's 'Walk on the Wild Side,' and she'd done lots of other backup work). But Culture Club made excellent use of her Aretha-like power. Jon even told the papers, 'To find a woman singer who could fit in with the band is incredible, and Helen's heaven-sent. She's perfect, she's a bit eccentric, she's not exactly what we call a "dolly bird," and she's got a great personality. She's fantastic, y'know, she's actually got her type of sex appeal.'

The album was a much more emotional one than the first one had been – maybe because Culture Club's initial success allowed George to be happier, to show his feelings more. Whatever the cause, show them he did. On 'It's a Miracle,' the refrain goes: 'And dreams are made of emotion – it's a miracle!' It's obvious that George's dreams are made of emotion. For a photo that ran in *Melody Maker* around the time, the Boy posed with his favourite stuffed animal – which he always takes on tour with him. He's not afraid to show how childlike he can be.

Colour By Numbers established Boy George –

not as a personality; everyone already knew he was that. And not as a singer; it was more than obvious he was that. It established him as a *songwriter*, and suddenly he was flooded with offers to write songs for or with other artists. He declined all of them except one: He wrote 'Mischief' for Tina Turner.

He also declined Prince Charles. Charles and Diana host a big benefit concert called The Prince's Trust about twice a year to raise money for young British musicians. Only the biggest British acts have played the Prince's Trust – last year Duran Duran flew back from recording in Australia at Charles and Diana's request. A royal invitation is nothing to sneeze at, and it's considered a command of sorts. Well, when George was approached – somewhat indirectly, since his manager, Tony Gordon, received the invitation – he merely replied that Culture Club would be too busy touring, that they couldn't disappoint their fans – and that he was terribly insulted that the prince hadn't asked him personally. 'He never asked *me*,' George sniffed dramatically. The British press found this very funny. But what was really funny about it is that the Boy could afford to say no.

But Boy George did not turn down an invitation from Joan Rivers to have tea, right after *Colour By*

Numbers came out. Joan was coming to England and wanted to meet the Boy everybody was talking about; she was thinking of having him come on the *Tonight* show with her.

The two had a lovely tea, and George felt like he could trust Joan to do a 'fun' interview with him. Sure enough, he appeared on the show in February of 1984 – which was perfect timing, becuse, by that time, most of America was aware of who Boy George was and was quite curious to get a better look.

George did not seem at all nervous. He was wearing an oversized multicoloured top, which he announced had been a bedspread in Barcelona, and that he'd just *had* to have it. The only touchy moments came when Joan Rivers interrogated him on his sexuality:

Joan: Which do you like – boys or girls?
George: You, darling!
Joan: No, *really*.
George: Well, either one . . . I don't really have time to think about that these days . . .

He was charming, he was witty, and almost most impressive about Boy George on the *Tonight* show was how impressed Joan Rivers was with the Boy.

He was a perfect foil for her brand of wild, dishy comedy, and he was every bit as subtly bitchy as she. The two really dished the dirt. All over America, viewers – young, old, middle-aged – were smiling and wondering 'Whatever made us dislike *him*? He's so . . . cute!'

Meanwhile, in an interview with MTV in the spring, George said this of his new friend Joan Rivers: 'I really admire her comedy . . . because, you know, women in England just don't tell those kind of jokes. I think she did the same for English comedy as I've done for American sexuality, you know! Made it feel quite out of date in a way.'

It was only a matter of time – a week or more – after George's appearance on the *Tonight* show that 'Karma Chameleon' went to number one on the *Billboard* charts. There was absolutely no more problem about Boy George making it in America.

Meanwhile, Culture Club was monstrously huge all over Europe, and the band was getting used to touring there, even though none of them – George, Mikey, Jon, or Roy – had ever set foot outside of England before they'd formed the band. George became an 'experienced' traveller very fast – being both observant and extemely opinionated about things he's only dealt with a short time. His travelling observances are very funny, particularly because our Boy never left England before he was in the band and because he's always hated travelling, never wanted to leave England, *still* hates travelling, and still doesn't really like leaving home. George also hates flying. He'll do it when he has to, but he's never felt good about it.

George seems to dislike playing in France more than anywhere else. 'The French are very rigid,' he announced after playing there a few times. 'And the French hate the English. We sold a million singles there, and they still don't come to see us play! I guess that's because France doesn't have a pop history, apart from Piaf. Perhaps society there is more agricultural. In France, they seem self-centred, they don't want to idolize us. I think they miss so many wonderful clichés because they're scared to seem uncool. I mean, if I ordered coffee in Paris with my *meals*, they laughed at me!'

George isn't much more favourable about Holland. 'The Dutch are weird, they have an odd sense of humour.' He thinks that because when Culture Club went there to shoot a TV show, the studio was arranged to look like an operating room – for 'Do You Really Want to Hurt Me.' That really pissed him off. 'Also, there are too many hippies in Amsterdam, and it's too laid back there, all the drugs.' George doesn't like drugs at all, and especially doesn't like anybody to take them when they're working with him.

'In Germany,' he recounted, 'we were in a restaurant, and this girl came up to me with a huge plate full of cocaine, and stuck it in my face and said "Hi!" ' George was very disgusted by this, thought it very rude, and said to her, 'The first thing for you to do is say hello properly.' 'I nearly blew it all off the plate,' he recalls. 'The other boys were laughing because they knew what it was. They said there was about three thousand dollars' worth. I seem to attract drug types in Europe.'

George did not like or approve of what he considered the sexual aggressiveness of the German women. 'It surprised me and shocked me,' he said, 'I once got stuck in a TV studio on my own. All these women trapped me, sticking their tits in my face and asking me to sign them! If a bloke told me to sign his crotch, I'd punch him in the mouth. They were lucky they were women.'

George's memories of Italy are really cursory. 'All I remember about Italy,' he says, 'is the noise and the history. Italy is mad! I don't understand it at all.'

George, does, however, have very detailed impressions of the European fashions he observed.

'The French are more androgynous and baggy in their clothes than in the rest of Europe – but I still don't go for European fashions. They tend to be very chauvinist. The idea of purveying sexuality in clothes is loathesome. I detest male fashions like that. Italian men think they're gorgeous – y'know, the gold medallion brigade. For some reason, I won an Italian men's fashion competition – they said my look was the tops. I couldn't believe that.'

Interestingly enough, it was around the time that 'Karma Chameleon' became a big hit that the 'Boy George look' *really* took off. Trendsetters in every country were already more than aware of it and had worn it to death already. But the American fashion industry has never been known for its originality or quickness to catch on. In winter of 1984, the stores – and not just in New York or L.A. – were suddenly lined with racks of big, shapeless 'things' (not dresses, not smocks), and were selling black hats by the barrelful. 'Boy George's oversized, raggedy, poverty-stricken look is really in, and it's the biggest influence for clothes this spring,' said one fashion expert at the National Fashion and Boutique Show in New York, in February 1984.

Here's George's own description of 'the Culture Club look': 'It's basically workman's fabrics, with provocative patterns. A very clean, very spiritual, very unsexy look. It is comprised of symbols which represent all the peoples that are looked down on. It's not stagewear, however. It's the way I live, and we take advantage of it without pretence.'

Meanwhile, back in Britain, Boy George was honoured by his own country with a wax figure of himself at Madame Tussaud's in London. That's the world-famous wax museum that did lifelike statuettes of the Beatles in the sixties. 'We took them out a little while ago, because we thought they'd become rather dated,' a spokesperson for Tussaud's said about the Beatles. The Boy George figure was an attempt to give the museum a newer image. The only other rock acts with wax figures there are David Bowie and Elton John. George, of course, was extremely pleased with the idea of being sculpted in wax – and even agreed to sit for designers without his make-up. However, the museum was *sworn* to secrecy about what he looks like without it, even though they had to take photos of him barefaced, George's personal clothing designeer of spring 1983 (they change from time to time), Dexter Wong, designed a special outfit, and a British sculptor named Judy Craig was hired to mix dyes, to get the make-up of the statue as colourful as George's. The wax model was unveiled in a big ceremony in spring of 1984 – an almost ultimate tribute to the future historical presence of a one-time black sheep.

At the same time, Boy George was named 'Best Rock Personality of 83' by the London *Daily Mirror.* He also won countless music paper awards as 'best dressed,' 'best male singer,' 'best female singer,' and so on. But the most prestigious British award given to Culture Club in 1983 was the British Phonographic Industry award for 'Best Group of the Year.' That's the equivalent of the Grammy and is a pretty serious honour. George, pleased as he was, was getting pretty used to awards at this point – dubious and otherwise. When he accepted the BPI award with Mikey, Jon, and Roy, he wasn't very serious at all – or *was* he? 'First of all,' the Boy pronounced, 'I'd like to say two things – one, I'm *not* a transvestite, and two, I *don't wear dresses.*' The British recording industry was taken aback – but not all that surprised. George swept off the stage, lifting the hem of his extremely long . . . smock.

Boy George's best awards acceptance speech had to be on the American Grammys, where Boy and band and Joan Rivers were telecast in March of 1984 by satellite. Their first appearance was to announce the winner of an award; their second was to accept the Grammy for Best New Band of the Year. They were pretty much a shoo-in; why else would the show have gone to the expense of satelliting them? 'Thanks a lot, America,' George said, smiling sweetly. 'You've got taste – you've got style – and you know a good drag queen when you see one!' It was a greatly humorous moment, but it contradicted everything George had ever said about his sexuality in interviews. He's always said he's *not* a transvestite or drag queen of any sort. 'That Boy George' was the common sentiment the day after. 'What a character!' No one seemed to be offended.

After the Grammy show, George was on British television and was queried as to why he referred to himself as a drag queen. 'I don't see myself as a drag queen,' he said. 'No one laughs at priests because they wear dresses. Their clothes are accepted. I'd eventually like society to accept the way I look that easily too. I'm not a woman. I'm a man. When I go to the bathroom every morning, I look at myself, and I'm in no doubt of that.'

8

VIDEO CULTURE

Culture Club videos, particularly the early ones, shocked a lot of people (George's mixed sexual messages, multi-ethnic back-up singers, wild clothing). During a London interview in 1983 that was being taped for MTV, George announced, with characteristic bravado, 'I think our videos are *awful* – they're *dreadful*. I don't *like* making videos. I don't like videos at all, really – they keep people from talking to each other. I'd rather just sit round a piano with friends than watch videos – and I'd rather be on a chat show, talking to people, than have them see our videos.' He had a lot of nerve saying this in an MTV interview. But then, Culture Club's videos have done so well on that channel that MTV couldn't afford to take offence.

The seven videos that have been seen in the U.S. – *Do You Really Want to Hurt Me, Time (Clock of the Heart), I'll Tumble 4 Ya, Church of the Poison Mind, Karma Chameleon, It's a Miracle*, and *Miss Me Blind* – all have one major thing in common – humour. (One, *Victims*, directed by the English video team Godley and Creme in the winter of 1983, hasn't been released over there, because the single wasn't released.) Perhaps due to George's attitude about video, there is a gentle flirtation with the camera that says 'We're having fun with this, please don't take it seriously.'

The *Do You Really Want to Hurt Me* video stirred up a bit more controversy in the States than in England. It did not appear on MTV originally. When the song started to get big in the U.S., MTV naturally began to feature it – but not the video the band had made for the song. They aired a clip from a live performance of Culture Club performing the song on England's *Top of The Pops* show.

The actual concept video itself, which had aired in England and had been playing all over the States in the rock video clubs, featured George, in his religious-lettered smock with white pants, braided locks, and his scarf and hat, as an entertainer at various posh London establishments (like dinner clubs and pool clubs). However, he keeps getting stared at by the patrons, as if a criminal – and he gets thrown out of all of them. Finally he's thrown into jail and goes to trial. He asks the jury if they 'really want to hurt' him, and their answer is to toss him into a cell. He sits, locked up and dejected, in solitary confinement – until a trio of Jamaican back-up singers mysteriously procures the key and frees him. Then he joins his waiting band and becomes the singer he wants to be.

What was so controversial about this video that MTV wouldn't play it? It's hard to say. However, about a month or so after the song became a hit, suddenly the concept video was in rotation. Then – *heavy* rotation. MTV's viewers wanted to see more of him and had no problem with the video.

Director Julien Temple (who directed the Sex Pistols' movie, *The Great Rock 'n' Roll Swindle*, and who's directed video clips for the Kinks, Dexy's Midnight Runners, ABC, and the Rolling Stones) says he came up with the concept for *Do You Really Want to Hurt Me* this way:

'I knew George for years, from hanging out in clubs. I liked the way he dressed and all; I thought he was like the Little Prince – you know, that sweet character in Saint-Exupéry's novel who's from another planet. George was well-known in the clubs, but outside of that situation, he was treated like a time traveller or something.

'The idea of putting him, even in a video, in the

Gargoyle Club in London was so outrageous – it's a very famous club, the one in the video. Lots of even famous people have been thrown out of that club. I wanted to put him in a setting where, years ago, he quite literally probably *would* have been arrested. Then, when he goes on trial, I thought of George *constantly* having to go on trial – in lots of ways – for being *himself*. Now he's accepted, and the idea would be passé.

'George really liked the idea. He asked me to do his next video, *Time*, but I was too busy. But I *really* like George – he's a witty guy, really lovely. He's grown into this nice image – he's become so *cuddly*. And I think that video conveyed that, along with all the nasty stuff people thought about him at the time.'

Time (Clock of the Heart), directed by Chris Gabrin for Limelight Productions, 'was good fun,' says Mikey Craig. This is his favourite Culture Club clip. 'It was very childish. It's George's creation – it's *good*, it's *warm*. Again, it has that family feel George needs to have – he needs to be secure, and he likes the family set-up. All four of us are sitting round drinking coffee and everybody's cup has got their name on it – "Mikey," "Boy," "Jon," and "Roy"; and the mum brings the cake in, and puts it down, and we're on the telly, and she goes, "Ooohhhhh!" '

Time conveys the complete opposite image of the band from their first clip, *Do You Really Want to Hurt Me.* It shows them in lovely new clothes, performing in a television studio – all proper and legit; and then in a living room watching the broadcast of their TV appearance. What's 'homey' about it is that you see the members of the band as everyday people, just sitting around with the folks – and you think, Wow, they're pretty normal, after all.

Director Chris Gabrin (who's made clips for Madness, John Cougar, Heaven 17, and the Thompson Twins) says he got the idea from talking to George and learning that one of the Boy's favourite activities is sitting at home and watching TV. He ends the video with a close-up of George, winking, 'because that's something George does naturally. I wanted to show him being slightly flirty – not dangerous, though.'

This time MTV played the video *before* the song went top ten – which it did, very soon after the video became a hit.

I'll Tumble 4 Ya, directed by Zelda Barron for Limelight Productions, features the Culture Club as good-natured vaudevillians who literally *do* tumble (albeit lightly) on the stage of a London dance hall. All the members of the band had to be given special dance lessons. The clip was *supposed* to be directed by veteran video director Steve Barron, but, due to scheduling problems, he couldn't do it. Then Limelight Video (a production house that's made many of the English and American video clips) suggested that maybe Steve's *mother*, Zelda Barron, might direct. Although not exactly a rock 'n' roller, she is a veteran movie-business person, has been an associate producer for many films (including *Coal Miner's Daughter* and *Continental Divide*), and was more than capable. George loved the idea of working with the feisty Zelda.

'Oh – *I'll Tumble* _ lovely!' she recalls of the experience. 'I *loved* doing that one. I thought they were joking when they suggested I direct it – I'd never actually *made* a film before, although I'd been in the background of a lot of them. Steve (my son) told me George would love it if I directed. So I heard the record – no one gave me ideas – and I thought it had a tap dance sort of melody. George *loved* that idea! He loves the idea of not appearing like a rock 'n' roller. I wrote a little script – which never actually happened – because of cutting. We didn't have much time to do it – it's so quick when you do a video – there isn't even enough time to get on anyone's nerves. I quickly learned that working with musicians is vastly different than working with actors. Musicians just don't care about the camera.

'The choreographer we used on *I'll Tumble* was Jillian Gregory – she taught Nureyev in *Valentino*! Culture Club loved that and liked the idea of learning how to do dance steps. George dropped out of the lessons first – he liked his little hop, and he says he can't dance. Mikey, Jon, and Roy did quite well in rehearsals, but then when it came to the shoot, they didn't do all *that* well. They got into the idea of sending themselves up. They do like to do that. I got even, I learned how to send them up – I developed a brilliant imitation of George in a bad temper! But he did say he liked *I'll Tumble* – in fact, he told me it was his favourite video.'

I'll Tumble 4 Ya was a particular hit with George's older fans (yes, including the 'grannies' he loves) because it has such a nostalgic feel for pre-rock 'n' roll entertainment.

Church of the Poison Mind, directed by Chris Gabrin for Limelight Productions, was the first video to be shot for the Culture Club's second album, *Colour By Numbers*. And George wanted it to be literally more colourful than anything they'd done so far.

The video is a slightly scrambled montage of London scenarios: It follows the band, as George sings – decked out in elaborate white clothing – in an open car that's driving around town. As the band is driving, waving, and singing, a couple of Japanese photographers pop out of the back seat. 'George told me, "There are Japanese photographers popping up wherever we go now!" – so I took him at his word,' says director Chris Gabrin. The photographers follow the boys to a picture shooting where they discover, to their shock, a large gang of girls who are all dressed like George – *exactly* like George! 'There were so many Boy George clones at that point that were girls, we thought it funny to feature them,' says Gabrin. 'The one we spotlighted and did a close-up on wasn't a fan, though. She's George's sister, Siobhain.'

Then there are shots of the band performing outside (the first clip that vocalist Helen Terry was seen in), and the final scenes of the clip are in an airplane, which Jon and Roy pilot, and the band is flying to the U.S. There's no telling *what* the 'Church of the Poison Mind' actually *is*, from the video, although George says the song is 'about how people get trapped by their own emotions. It's based on the Japanese idea that the brain is the temple of the body. I'm saying every relationship is a new experience, and you should take everything as it comes, and not be trapped by the church of the poison mind.' The video is more like a brief history of Culture Club's whirlwind success, and of that car driving around London with the band, Chris Gabrin will only say, 'Oh, the car? Just a device to get the band from one place to another. If you think how quickly the band's travelled in terms of success, they should have been flying around London. Maybe that's why I had them flying at the end.'

'Karma Chameleon' was Culture Club's first number-one song in the U.S., and its accompanying video, directed by Peter Sinclair for Limelight Productions, has also been the band's most popular so far. Maybe that's because it's the first to actually have a sort-of story line.

The song has a countryish sound, so it was decided that the video would *look* like it was shot on a riverboat going down the Mississippi. The 'karma chameleon' in it is a thief who's a pick-pocket on the boat and who spoils everyone's fun. The crowds are all dressed in 'red, gold, and green'

– the colours in the song. At the end, everything works out okay, becquse the chameleon is forced to walk the plank. Boy George is a bit separate from the action, because he's sitting on top of the boat, singing.

Zelda Barron recounts the shooting of *Karma Chameleon*: 'I had to shoot a film during *Karma*, but I wrote the script for it, and Peter Sinclair directed. I suggested the riverboat – it went in a different direction than my original idea, though. It always does!

'Nothing went particularly right on this shoot – it was the worst in Limelight's history, I think. They shot it on the Thames, with Siobhan [Siobhan Barron, Zelda's daughter, who runs Limelight] basically in charge. Jillian Gregory choreographed again, as in *Tumble*.

'But some of the dancers got lost and never turned up! Siobhan had to take one of their places; she's that Ava Gardner-looking one. She wasn't too happy about that, you can believe it. There were camera problems, too. No one was speaking to each other at the end of the day. Luckily, it's a good song, so the video didn't kill it!'

You'd never know there were so many problems to look at *Karma Chameleon* – and, according to MTV and various video clubs around the country, it was Culture Club's biggest video hit to date.

To this date, *It's a Miracle*, directed by Zelda Barron for Limelight Productions, hasn't been released in the U.S., because the band's U.S. label, Epic Records, decided to release 'Miss Me Blind' as the single instead. Therefore no one in America has seen the *It's a Miracle* video yet – and won't see it until Culture Club releases a video album, at some undetermined date in the future. So here's Zelda's description of it:

'This is my favourite Culture Club video. It's a big board game, set on the lines of Monopoly – but it's the history of Culture Club. George, Roy, Mikey, and Jon hop along to different squares, and when they land, you see bits from all their other promo videos. It's less technical than *Miss Me Blind* and really for the band's fans. You get to see just how they got to be where they are now. And – it's all a game, and really fun. If only it was that way!'

Miss Me Blind, directed by Zelda Barron for Limelight Productions, is Culture Club's 'arty' video. The 'blind' part of *Miss Me Blind* is taken quite literally, and there are a lot of windows, with blinds being drawn or lifted throughout the clip. And very often George is behind one – with his new hairdo (no braids, but long curled hair), wearing a kimono and very Japanese make-up. The action seems to take place in a pagoda, where a geisha and some Japanese warriors are preparing for a ceremony. The members of the band are lost and seemingly looking for an also-lost George (is that why they 'miss' him?). It's completely unclear what's going on, but George looks so great in this one, everyone wants to see it. Zelda fills in the details:

'We *all* did the script for this one – me, Steve, and George. George is getting very good at videos, much better than he'd give himself credit for. The ideas just rattle out of him. He also does all the clothes in the videos – he designs them all. That's one of the best things about these videos, George's clothes. He also has done his own hair and make-up for all of them.

'*Miss Me Blind* is the most technical video I've done. The lighting alone took so much time. It was lit by Jack Cardiff, who lit *The Red Shoes* and was a cameraman on *The African Queen*. This was his first promo – and he really enjoyed himself. In fact, he's writing a book about all his film work now, and he's calling it *From Gish to George*. The lighting was great. Too bad we posterized [filled the screen with many blocks of the same image] the clip in the end; that's the reason it looks so . . . odd. George is the only thing in the clip that isn't posterized.

'I think this is the last Culture Club clip for me – probably my last clip for good. As much as I enjoy doing them – I don't! I'm going back to film work, and Culture Club doesn't need me anymore. George is full of great ideas – his ideas are incredible. I told him *he* should direct his own videos, and he said, "Zelda, I've been thinking of it." I wouldn't be at all surprised to see that happen in the near future.'

A progression from videos to films was a likely one for Culture Club. But not as actors – as soundtrack writers and musicians. The film *Electric Dreams* (set for release in the summer of 1984) was a big step for George and the band and opened up new doors for them.

Video director Steve Barron – who's known for Michael Jackson's *Billie Jean*, the Human League's *Don't You Want Me*, and countless other clips – was asked to direct his first feature film in the winter of 1983. He needed original songs for the soundtrack, and he didn't want to use instrumental ones. He wanted songs that could make it in the pop world but could also hold up in a film. He'd really liked all of Culture Club's songs and had a feeling they might be right for the project. This is how the connection happened:

'I first met George when I visited the set of Culture Club's video *I'll Tumble 4 Ya* – my mother, Zelda, was directing,' Barron recounted. 'I knew I was going to direct this film, which was backed by Virgin Records, George's label. So I asked him to read the script, thinking he wouldn't take it seriously, doing film music. But he read it four times, and loved the emotion – George loves a love story, and he particularly liked this one, where a guy and his computer fall in love with the same girl.

'When George gets excited about something, he bubbles over with ideas. So that's what happened here – he wrote three songs practically right away. Then the band completed the tracks for them – "Love Is Love," "The Dream," and "Hello Goodbye Song." Now they think the songs are the best they've ever written or recorded.

'I don't think George has just matured as a songwriter – "Do You Really Want to Hurt Me" was a mature song. I think he and the band have maintained their quality, which is often harder than growing. I know they'll be around a long time – they've got great consistency. The band writes most of the music, George writes the lyrics, and there's a collective fusion that's great. There isn't a song of theirs I haven't liked. That's why I'll be directing their next three videos.'

Producer Rusty Lemorande, who produced *Caddyshack* and *Yentl*, was a lot less familiar with the British pop music world than Steve Barron, but decided to let Barron have a go at using Boy George because it could mean a lot of extra publicity for the film (and it has).

'George was the first musician approached for the soundtrack of *Electric Dreams*, and I was a bit sceptical about him,' said Lemorande. 'The last thing I expected from Boy George was concern about the lyrics of the songs and that they relate to the script – which is just about the most important thing about film songs.

'Well, George wasn't too keen on the idea of doing a movie, but he loved this script. He got so involved with it, in fact, that his lyrics seemed almost *psychic* about the plot. George's concern with dialogue in the script was equal to that of major film lyricists. But with these songs, they don't *have* to be heard in the context of the film to be appreciated.

'George was so excited about the songs right after he first started work on them, he taped himself singing the lyrics and brought the tape over to me and Steve. We sat in my car, and he played the tape on a small cassette player and sang the backing tracks out loud. Sure enough, some Culture Club fans were passing by and went completely crazy!

'Well, I was so pleased with the songs lyrically that I rewrote a whole scene to fit "Hello Goodbye" – the lyrics are among the most sophisticated I've worked with. George actually took the script a whole step further, if you ask me. I'm hoping I can actually do a whole musical with him at some point – write it and produce it with him. George kept emphasizing to me throughout the film that he thinks of himself as a *songwriter* first and a singer second.

'I know so many people who are impressed with his songs – even Barbra Streisand has been after me to introduce her to George; she wants to record one of his songs. But I hope he'll do more film work, and after *Electric Dreams*, he says he wants to. Unfortunately, most of the scripts George is getting sent now are for acting jobs people want him to do. And I don't think he wants to do those. But a big stage musical – maybe next year!'

9

YOU'RE A BIG BOY NOW

It was late autumn of 1983, and an editor of *Musician* magazine was asking Keith Richards in an exclusive interview what records he was into now. The editor expected to hear not about new records but ones by soul and reggae giants like Muddy Waters and Bob Marley. Richards said he hated Prince, was a bit tired of the Police, thought Joan Jett, Aztec Camera, and Talking Heads were all pretty good. His favourite record at the moment, though, was by Culture Club — the *Colour By Numbers* album. 'Boy George is good,' he said, relatively impressed. '*Real* good. I'd rate him an eight and a half out of ten.'

It became a *joke* in the British newspapers how many critics, celebrities, and music people were saying 'And you know Boy George – he can really *sing*!' – as if that might be an odd feat. But it was true, the second album certified our Boy as a real credible talent. 'Credible' has less to do with sales and hype and the public, and more to do with the judgment of the musical community itself.

George was flooded with even more offers to write songs and record duets with people. He still turned them all down, except for the three new songs for Steve Barron's *Electric Dreams*. He'd worked with Zelda Barron on many of the Culture Club videos and felt comfortable with the Barron brigade. He trusted Steve's idea that Culture Club songs would be right for the upcoming romantic comedy and took the whole project very seriously. They would be the next three songs on Culture Club's third album.

But meanwhile, the Boy and his Clubbers were *so* well liked by the press, so outside the realm of prejudice in terms of record sales, that it was pretty hard to believe they'd only a year before been considered so outlandish, even dangerous. Was it the band that had changed? Or was it the nature of the music business? Or was it the club scene itself?

In England, a lot of George's old clubbing chums were very jealous, claiming outright that he borrowed from their fashion sensibility, that they'd influenced him – that he wasn't the only good-looking cross-dresser in the London clubs. Perhaps they were right. But then why didn't *they* have the big record contracts? Why didn't they write great songs?

For the moment, the danger's gone out of the London club scene. The music business is now extracting every dressed-up person from the hub and sticking them in front of talented, not-so-flamboyant back-up singers and going for the hits. Many of Boy George's old hangouts are now tourist traps. Duran Duran, the slick pop band that started up around the same time, is highly competitive with them and issues less-than-kind statements in *New Musical Express* and *Melody Maker* about Culture Club's supposed commercialism. Boy's old friends, Jeremy Fantayzee (who's disbanded Hayzi Fantayzee), and new-cult-item Marilyn, who feels he can dethrone George by acting more feminine than the Boy, seem to have turned against him. George and group don't much seem to care. In *Melody Maker* in December 1983, George made these comments about their sudden press backlash and their very fast success:

'It's pathetic, but you can't let it bother you. I've got hundreds of pictures of Jeremy which are hilarious, but I would never be as childish as he is to print them – but, y'know, who cares? *I'm* not desperate for money, *I'm* not a one-hit wonder, so I don't need to sell pictures of people. No, really, I try not to be bitchy, but you can't help it sometimes, you fall into that kind of trip of being spiteful about people, and I just hate it. I mean, I've never wanted to answer any of the rude comments Duran Duran have made about me, I don't want to be a part of it. I don't feel part of any British invasion, I don't feel part of the pop scene, I don't mix with rock stars, and I don't think I've got anything in common with anyone like that.'

And have they changed any, as a result of all of this?

'Meeting George really changed me,' Jon Moss told the *Melody Maker* in the same issue. 'I've got wealthy parents, right, so I suppose it's a corny thing to say, but I was a middle-class angry young man, and I didn't really know what I wanted to do – but meeting George changed me. He was really wild, and I was quite conservative, and we balanced each other out perfectly.'

Yes, the band members all work together quite nicely now, although when they started, they had a reputation for brutal arguments, even somewhat violent ones. 'We understand each other now,' says Mikey. 'The fighting's cooled out, it's easier to be together because we're successful. We discuss things in a civilized way.'

'It's like a family, it really is,' says Jon of the entire Culture Club organization. 'I mean, sometimes I still want to kill George when he's haughty – then I'll go away for two days, and miss him like my girlfriend or something. We're all really close.'

George might have remained good friends with old friends, and very close to all the members of the band and the Culture Club organization – but it was true that he and other present and ex-pop stars were not quite seeing eye to eye. When Siouxsie and the Banshees' bassist Steve Severin reviewed singles in the *Melody Maker*, he wasn't very kind to 'It's a Miracle,' the song that was released in England when 'Miss Me Blind' was released in the States. 'I don't think Boy George can say anything worthwhile anymore. He's too big and safe.' It was a relatively cheap shot, since Siouxsie and the Banshees are very popular within London's avant-garde but have never been known to sell a wealth of records.

George, 'big' as he may be, was not about to take this sitting down. He wrote his own letter back to the *Melody Maker*. He put down the Banshees for 'negative song lyrics' and said, 'Don't talk to me about fake stardom. Because you and the other so-called punk heroes are just waiting to be put out to pasture.'

Culture Club had just sold four million albums worldwide, and Boy George didn't feel threatened by anyone. He was finally in the only position in which he could be comfortable: international stardom. It became thoroughly commonplace to see fans cloning his look. After the April 1984 tour, he went back to England and told his friends he'd seen redneck truckers in the South (male, of course) wearing dresses at his concerts!

During the American football season, a Boy George lookalike contest was even held at a Detroit Pistons game during halftime! It was only one of hundreds, but it couldn't have been held at a more unlikely place. Even *Playboy* magazine ran their own Boy George lookalike contest. The winner was comedian John Candy.

He even showed up in the 'Brenda Starr' comic strip, which is syndicated to hundreds of newspapers across the U.S. Brenda goes to a rock concert, and what is the band onstage playing but 'Karma Chameleon.'

George's look caught on so big, all kinds of American clothes manufacturers started using labels in their garments that might make kids on Melrose Avenue in Los Angeles or West Broadway in New York think they were Boy George's own label. Some were called Boy and used Culture

Club-looking symbols; some claimed to be the official label of the band but made hats and fake dreadlocks that barely approximated the authentic Boy George look.

George himelf was complimented by all this imitation, but he thought designers were charging exorbitant amounts of money for *his* look, and mostly because his name was supposedly on it. So George came up with another one of his schemes, Common Currency. That's the name of the line of clothes he started designing in England in March of 1984. He announced that the clothes would look very much like the outfits he himself wears, but wouldn't be very expensive – the pieces are not meant to sell for more than thirty-five or forty dollars apiece. They were also meant to be in U.S. stores during the summer of 1984. But in the band's only U.S. press conference, in Atlanta last April, George announced he was *not* designing clothes. He said Common Currency was only meant for the band to wear – but this remains to be seen.

Boy-mania was cropping up in other areas as well. On February 3, 1984, *U.S.A. Today* ran an article entitled 'Sexuality Slips Into Neutral Gear.' Amid a recounting of the 'gender-bender' phenomenon – from Boy to Annie Lennox of Eurythmics to the film *Liquid Sky* – it told of a not-so-typical incident at one high school:

'It was not the usual adolescent argument. Two Lansing, Michigan, high school athletes recently steamed up the locker room debating the masculinity of Boy George.

'Boys will be boys. Today, some boys will be Boy George. The lead singer of the British New Wave/soul group Culture Club has grabbed national attention as much for his make-up as his music. No stranger to dresses, powder, and eyeliner, he is most commonly described as "androgynous." '

Strictly defined, androgyny is the merging of male and female characteristics. These days, it's a look that sometimes makes us ask Is it a man or a woman? Androgyny may not be sweeping the nation, but it has become a hot topic of conversation.

An English magazine announced that the age of the 'gender-bender' was upon us – that androgyny was finally here, finally accepted, that all the so-called boundaries between the sexes were being broken down. 'The gender-benders, as they call them, have spread far and wide, from the small in-clubs of Soho and Covent Garden, and can now be found – along with post-punks in parakeet plumage, rude boys with stingy-brims, and unreconstructed punks with tartan diapers trailing – in every small town in the realm.'

In England, gender-benders – anybody with attributes of a sex other than their own – have been thought highly trendy for years. But in the U.S., all it takes is one spiked bracelet to raise an eyebrow, outside of New York City nightclubs. How much has Boy George affected the breakdown, and re-building, of sexual stereotypes and nonstereotypes in America's present culture? Well, first of all, pop music is where kids get all their major examples. And kids have taken to the Boy with absolutely no problem whatsoever – never needing to question his look, only finding it interesting, flamboyant, and the modern equivalent of the extremes of the rock 'n' roll look.

Here's a letter that was printed in the April 1984 issue of *Star Hits*, the American number-one pop magazine for teenagers:

> I love Boy George. He's the greatest! Even my two-year-old niece walks around singing 'Karma Chameleon.' I admire the Boy for having enough guts to dress the way he does. My friends think I'm crazy, but I think he is extremely sexy and very beautiful! Boy George, I feel the same way you do, and I quote, 'Clothes do not make the man.' I think your courage is proof enough that you're a real man.
>
> – Boy George Girl, Louisiana

This one's from the July 1984 issue:

> I'm a thirty-three-year-old woman, reasonably intelligent in every way, thank you. I also think Boy George is the sexiest man I've ever laid eyes on. Sorry, can't give you my name, but my teenage son would have a fit.
>
> – Charleston, West Virginia

What are George's thoughts on all of this? He has made about a thousand statements relating to the subject of gender at this point – but he never really gives a *straight* answer. For instance, when asked if he was heterosexual, he answered plainly, 'I don't believe *anyone* is heterosexual, *that* idea is a load of crap. I'm not interested in gay rights, because to me, gay is *normal*. It's being free to do what you want to do. I'm not one of those people who could go on a march in support of gay rights. I don't want to get involved with a tribe. I'm an individual, and I want everybody to take me as I am. I don't apologize for being me.'

He also *insists* that he is highly moral. 'I'm not a scandalous person. I would never sell my sex life to the papers. Everyone I've loved, I'll love till I die. I have very traditional ideas about sexuality and love. I fall in love twenty-four hours a day – I think people should fall in love a lot, it's healthy. I always go out with really nice people, and I really love all of them. I *don't* go out with people for the sake of having sex. It's too messy to have people like that in your life. I used to do all that, years ago. Now I can't be bothered.'

George admits that he *enjoys* the ambiguity perceived in his sexuality. 'I don't *want* to draw the line as regards sexual personality. I don't want to be a he-man, or a simpering poof, they're equally disgusting and unappealing. I want people to say, "Is it a bird or a plane?" I want to keep shuffling my cards. People know, but they don't – that's the glamour.'

Well, there you are – the activity Boy George prefers – shuffling his sexuality, having the freedom from it to hide it sometimes and the courage to flaunt it at others. It obviously doesn't affect his morals or emotions in any way. Is this true sexual freedom – something to aspire to – or just a utopian idea that only a rock star could pull off? Well, our Boy seems to have been headed in this direction since the age of fourteen. Now, on second thought, is he a rock star because of his openness, his frankness, his originality of thought and beliefs? Certainly, a fresh emotion comes through on Culture Club songs.

This may be the biggest reason for the constant pairing of Boy George with Michael Jackson's name in the media. They've not been paired as a couple – except by the *National Enquirer* and other scandal sheets. But their success has been attributed to a sexually unthreatening and sexually mysterious nature that appeals to teenage boys and girls and to men and women of all ages. Also, Michael's name is very often paired with a lot of people's – like Thomas Dolby's, Freddy Mercury's (of Queen), Mick Jagger's, Paul McCartney's. Michael likes to sing duets. That's why he called up Boy George, in March of 1984 – to ask him about singing a duet with him, perhaps actually writing a song together. Although Michael and the Boy are on the same record label in the States – Epic – they'd never met before the phone call.

Within days, their conversation was quoted in both English and U.S. newspapers.

George told the papers this about rejecting – yes, *rejecting* – an offer from the world's biggest star: 'I do admire Michael. He's a genius, he really is – but I've never been one of his fans. I just don't want to work with anyone but Culture Club right now. I think we're the best band around, and I don't see anyone who could dethrone us.'

No one could believe George said no to Michael

Jackson – or felt that he could afford to. Neither could he, really. But then, he'd already pretty much rejected a similar offer from another admirer – Barbra Streisand. He met her through *Electric Dreams* and *Yentl* producer Rusty Lemorande but had to decline a request from her because, as the Boy said, 'I'm too busy right now – although I do now primarily see myself as a songwriter rather than a singer – and I'm sure I'll be writing songs for other people in the future. But not while I can sing them.'

And, the fact is, right after the Michael Jackson incident, U.K. papers announced that George could indeed afford to say no: Culture Club had broken a financial record that had been set by the Beatles. No, the members have hardly made more money than the Beatles in the three years they've been together. But they've made money at a *faster rate* than any band *since* the Beatles. Anyone who's over twenty-five will remember how fast the Beatles made it. Everyone else will just have to imagine that all the Culture Club boys have done pretty well in their three years' time.

Culture Club's spring 1984 North American tour was beyond anything they could have expected. They'd crossed the U.S. and Canada a number of times at this point, always doing reasonably well.

They'd played some very large halls. But they hadn't toured with this many hits behind them, and all the press attention, and – not the least of it – the American Grammy Award. And the most amazing thing about this tour was that it was a short one. The band wasn't even playing most of the major cities – primarily places across the South. They are waiting till autumn 1984, after they release their third album, to do their biggest tour, which will include New York's Madison Square Garden. But the response to the spring tour was still phenomenal.

When Culture Club arrived at Montreal airport on April 3, 1984, they were welcomed with a big surprise: three thousand people, screaming and going crazy. When George got off the plane, he asked the police to allow the fans to get as near to him as possible. Of course, despite George's good intentions, a riot ensued, and a dozen people got injured in the crunch – including a police officer, who fainted in the middle of the crowd. The Montreal concert, which opened the tour, proved to be a landmark event, with scalpers demanding up to three hundred dollars for tickets.

In Miami, tickets for a five-thousand-seat hall went on sale in March and sold out in four hours. Hundreds of kids waited in line for days, even sleeping outside the ticket centre. The scene was reminiscent of Beatles and Rolling Stones concerts nearly twenty years ago. When asked by a Miami *Herald* reporter why they were sleeping in line, kids gave the most logical answers:

'I don't know how old you are, but Boy George is like Elvis Presley was in your time. An idol. He's honest. He doesn't keep anything hidden. He's honest about his appearance.'

'Boy George is gonna be a legend.'

'Boy George is the standard everyone's being measured against.'

Variety, the entertainment world newspaper, picked it up in their April 4, 1984, issue: 'Not since the Beatles crossed the Atlantic, two decades back, has Montreal been so swept by such a rock 'n' roll frenzy. And, while mop-top Beatle haircuts were all the rage of a generation gone by, this newest mania takes the form of Boy George "gender bendering" as legions of fans adopt the androgynous look of Culture Club's outrageously attired lead singer.'

Britain's *Daily Mirror*, not known for understatement, was much more gushing about the spring 1984 tour: 'It is as though the Messiah himself has unexpectedly turned up at a revivalist meeting.'

Wherever they went – Montreal, Buffalo, Pittsburgh, Atlanta – the crowd started screaming the minute the Boy took the stage, and it never stopped. Girls were going crazy and guys were going crazy. Behind them, safely deposited a number of rows back, their mothers were screaming.

How could they possibly top themselves after this tour? By releasing two more records simultaneously – 'Believin' It All' and 'Love Lies Lost.' Both were written by Boy George and recorded by members of Culture Club, but neither are Culture Club songs. 'Believin' It All' is a record sung by Culture Club's producer, Steve Levine. He told George he wanted to sing his own song. George wrote him one. Of course, Steve produced. Meanwhile, since winter '83–'84, George, Roy, Mikey, and Jon have been writing and recording material for vocalist Helen Terry's first solo album. Her first song was 'Love Lies Lost.' George wrote it and sang backup vocals, with the Culture Club lineup throughout. George was obviously generous and supportive of those who'd been the same with him. He was keeping it a family affair.

In the summer of 1984, the band went into the studio to record their third album, tentatively called *Waking Up with the House on Fire*. George told the press that he got the title from a Doris Day movie. He didn't elaborate, but he did reveal that the mysterious lines of Japanese at the end of the 'Miss Me Blind' video with the guitars on fire can be translated as 'waking up with the house on fire.' That's George's way of introducing their next album. But then, he's woken up with his own life on fire.

In Atlanta last spring, Boy George was once again queried on the topic of his sexuality. He thought he'd said it all before, so he decided to give a definitive answer – and wound up delivering Culture Club's credo.

'I think rock 'n' roll has survived on sexuality for the last three decades. And what Culture Club is doing is not promoting sexuality. I mean, anybody who thinks sex risqué is very stupid. Sex is dull, old-fashioned. It's the same as taking drugs. And what Culture Club is promoting is a new kind of – you know – *acceptance*, in a way. I mean, five years ago, I would never have been able to do what I'm doing now. You know, when we were playing in Phoenix, Arizona, last year, there were kids of five. I think that kind of thing in the audience shows how powerful music and what we're doing has become. I think that there are a lot of people in the press who think we're corrupting young people – but in effect we're making them more intelligent. Because what we're doing is – we're telling them to be *themselves*. We're not telling them to look at us as some kind of demigod. You know, with a phallic symbol like a guitar, and tight jeans. We're telling them, you know, we're not perfect. We're dealing with much more interesting things than rock 'n' roll and sex. We're dealing with imperfections, we're dealing with things that go on in society. Things that affect *real* people.

'And that's why people like us. A lot of young kids – they're much more intelligent than you are. There was a little girl on the news in Detroit, who was thirteen. When they asked her what she thought of Boy George, she said, "Boy George is not telling men to be women and women to be men. He's saying do what you feel like." That's more intelligent than anyone could say.'

American journalist Merle Ginsberg started taking music and the music business seriously when she wrote for *The Soho News*, from 1980 to 1982. After that, she became a freelance arts writer and journalist, and has since written primarily about music and video for *New Musical Express, The Village Voice*, the *Daily News, The Record, Creem*, and *Heavy Metal*. For the last two years she's been a regular reporter for MTV's *Music News*, and recently wrote the script for MTV and Vestron's 'History of Videomusic.' She has begun work on a novel set in the club scene in New York.

THE ROLLING STONES

Roy Carr

The first complete guide to every Rolling Stones recording with an uncompromising pictorial diary of the Stones' careers, riots and incredible lifestyles. Compiled and written by *New Musical Express* Special Projects Editor ROY CARR (also co-author of THE BEATLES: AN ILLUSTRATED RECORD) with 200 illustrations, a diary of events, all possible recording details, and an interview with Mick Jagger.

NEW ENGLISH LIBRARY

THE BEATLES, AN ILLUSTRATED RECORD

Roy Carr & Tony Tyler

The first and only complete critical guide to all Beatles recordings. This is the famous, dazzling pictorial record of their lives and loves, quarrels and successes. Compiled and written by 'New Musical Express' editors Roy Carr and Tony Tyler, with 200 illustrations, a complete diary, selected quotes and interviews, and all possible recording details. This new edition includes the tragic death of John Lennon.

NEW ENGLISH LIBRARY

JOHN LENNON: ONE DAY AT A TIME

A Personal Biography of the Seventies by Anthony Fawcett

'This book is about the growth of the artist John Lennon, a poet, a primitive musician, and certainly a practical dreamer. John, as a mirror of our times, always innately felt the need to change, to search for new ideas, new experiences, new people. The idea of 'one day at a time' worked for John, as it does for many of us, not only to keep his own life in perspective but also to cope with the paraphernalia and visual jetsam which constantly assault our senses.

'In this book I have tried to understand the man, the artist, and his inner workings. If such an understanding is in some way communicated to the reader I will be satisfied.'

Anthony Fawcett

NEW ENGLISH LIBRARY

PLAYBOY INTERVIEWS WITH JOHN LENNON AND YOKO ONO

by David Sheff & Barry Golson

The Playboy interviews are the complete texts plus currently unpublished conversations and Lennon's own song-by-song analysis of his music. All the interviews were conducted in New York by David Sheff during the Autumn of 1980 before John Lennon was so tragically murdered on the 9th December of that year.

'In hindsight, what seemed undeniable to us in that autumn was that these interviews were something special to John Lennon. It was the first time in five years he and his wife, Yoko Ono, had spoken with the outside world, and he had stored up a lot of things to say. He was giving a few other, shorter interviews to promote their new record album, but the Playboy sessions, for whatever reasons, were evidently the means he had chosen to sum it *all* up – the Beatles, Paul McCartney, his own childhood, the seeds of rebellion and artistry, the creation of the music itself, the relationship with Yoko, and everything he'd come to learn about politics and sexual roles and creativity and passion – and why men of peace are inevitably gunned down.'

NEW ENGLISH LIBRARY

THE MICHAEL JACKSON STORY

by Nelson George

He's twenty-four and a superstar. Album after album, single after single, explode like supernova starbursts into the Top Ten. *Thriller*, the album, has worldwide sales of over 18,000,000. From the age of five when he first began singing with the Jackson 5, to his present-day solo domination, he has excited, enthralled and enraptured millions; on record, on video, on film and live on stage.

Paul McCartney, Diana Ross, Steven Spielberg, Jane Fonda and Brooke Shields are friends and professional colleagues. The gold and platinum dazzle of on-stage, up-front success glitters round him.

But when the lights dim and the crowds go out into the night, each with a little bit of the Michael Jackson magic in their hearts, where does *he* go? What are *his* dreams? What is the private world of the enchanter? Is he lonely as well as shy? Who are his true, trusted friends and his real loves?

The Michael Jackson Story takes you quietly by the hand and leads you into the heartland of his inner thoughts, his hopes, his family and his emotions.

NEW ENGLISH LIBRARY